Traditional Indian curry in a hurry

Babita Taneja and Win Dulai

foulsham
LONDON • NEW YORK • TORONTO • SYDNEY

foulsham

The Publishing House, Bennetts Close, Cippenham,
Slough, Berkshire, SL1 5AP, England

Dedication

*For our Mums and Dads, who are our greatest teachers of love, compassion
and living life with passion.*

*For our husbands, for their patience and excellent food-tasting abilities.
And for Krishan, for always entertaining us.*

ISBN-13: 978-0-572-03095-7
ISBN-10: 0-572-03095-9

Copyright © 2005 W. Foulsham and Co. Ltd

Cover photograph by The Anthony Blake Photo Library

Author photographs by Peter Howard Smith

Photographs by Stonecastle Grapics Ltd

A CIP record for this book is available from the British Library

Printed in Great Britain by St. Edmundsbury Press, Bury St. Edmunds, Suffolk

Contents

Introduction

Indian families see food as an integral part of their culture. This is most apparent through festivals, birthdays, weddings and religious community get-togethers, which usually involve the women in the family coming together – a major social event in itself! – the night before or at the weekend to cook on a massive scale for the family and guests.

We are both second-generation British Indian women who have been fortunate enough to have received from our mothers and aunties (who have well over 60 years of chapatti and curry-making experience) their passion and knowledge of food. They have taught us authentic recipes, which they in turn learned from their mothers and aunties, so that we too can cook terrific Indian family dishes using traditional recipes.

Many people, from every possible ethnic background, love Indian food and want to make authentic home-cooked Indian dishes but are afraid to attempt them in their own kitchens for fear they will be difficult and time-consuming. With this book, that's no longer an issue.

These recipes have been adapted by our mothers and by ourselves to fit in with our busy modern lifestyles, so our recipes allow readers to create and taste real Indian food as made within the homes of typical modern Indian families – and just as fast! We have captured and collected well over a hundred fantastic recipes that we would cook at home, but with the emphasis on simplicity, speed and using readily available ingredients.

Both our families originate from the Punjab in northern India, so most of our recipes are derived from dishes from that region. Punjabis are well known for their energy and passion, and that is demonstrated in their enthusiasm for food and the important contribution they have made to the vibrant world of Indian food.

Beyond our Indian roots we have also been influenced by our upbringing in Britain, growing up on mum's desi omelette, masala lamb chops, Indian eggy bread and cola milk, and dad's famous quick fish sabji.

Of course, most people know by now that there is no such word as 'curry' in any Indian language. It is a British term used to describe an Indian dish containing spices, a term that has now made it into English dictionaries as well as on to every possible restaurant menu. Because of this, we also use it, as it is recognised and established in Indian cooking in Britain and beyond.

We believe that once you have tasted a good home-made Indian curry, there will be no going back – you will be hooked! This book will enable you to create dishes with an authentic taste to give pleasure to your family and friends, as well as provide immense satisfaction in your cooking.

We have tried to ensure that all the ingredients we use are readily available, and most people will have no problem in obtaining them from their local supermarket or Asian store. However, for those who may prefer to buy online, we have included a valuable list of resources, including online mail order companies who sell and deliver spices direct to your home (see page 142).

We have given each of our recipes its own Punjabi title, and then included an English translation.

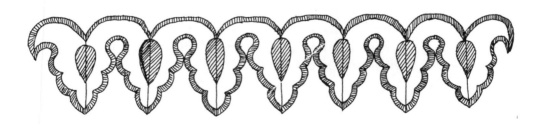

Your Indian Storecupboard

Most of the ingredients used in our recipes are now available in major supermarkets, but if you want to buy in Indian stores it will be useful to know their Indian names, so we've added them in brackets where they differ from the English/American names.

Don't be put off by the number of spices we've included. Most of them are inexpensive, especially if you do buy them from Indian stores; and as you won't want to buy them in huge quantities (they do keep very well but will eventually lose their pungency) they don't take up much room. In any case, dried spices look so attractive if displayed in your kitchen in small, clear or darkened glass jars on a shelf or a rack. If you do this, don't forget to label them, and include the date you bought them.

BASICS

Cans: black chick peas/black garbanzos (kale chole); chick peas/garbanzos (chole); coconut milk; mango (am); pilchards in tomato sauce; kidney beans (raj mah); tomatoes.

Flours: chapatti flour (atta), which comes in different varieties ranging from white to 100 per cent wholemeal; chick pea/garbanzo flour (besan), made from ground chick peas and usually described as gram flour on the packet (used as a basis for Indian snacks); cornflour/cornstarch; cornmeal (makki dah atta); self-raising/self-rising flour (maida).

Fresh vegetables and herbs: aubergine/eggplant (bengan); carrots (gajar); cauliflower (gobi); coriander/cilantro (dhainya); garlic (lassan); green finger chillies (hari mirch); lemons (nimbu); limes (nimbu); mint (pudina); okra/ladies' fingers (bhindi); onions (piyaz); potatoes (aloo); root ginger (adrak); spinach (palak).

Frozen: peas (matter), sweetcorn/corn (shaley) and other vegetables (sabji); lamb/soya mince (keema); white fish (machchi).

Oils: canned clarified butter (ghee) – can be bought pre-packed in 500 g containers (see On-line Resources, page 142); olive oil; sunflower or vegetable oil.

Packets: split yellow chick peas/garbanzos (chana dhal); creamed coconut (nariyal); dried kidney beans (raj mah); whole black lentils (mah dhal); split black lentils (urid dhal); whole brown lentils (moth dhal); whole green lentils (moong dhal); red lentils (masoor dhal); red cow peas (red moth dhal); split yellow lentils (moong dhal); unsalted cashew nuts (kaju); almonds (badam); pistachio nuts (pista); white basmati rice (chawal).

Extras: rose water (gulab jal); mint sauce (pudina); tamarind paste (imli); full-fat milk powder (gulab jaman powder).

SPICES

Bay leaves (tejpat): derived from the bay laurel tree and used in Indian food for their warm bouquet and flavour to lightly fragrance rice and meat dishes.

Brown cardamom (kali elachi): these big pods are much larger and more pungent than the green variety. Because of their stronger taste they are used in masala mixes, in meat and rice dishes, and for tea (chai).

Chillies (mirch): there are over 150 different varieties of chilli. The general rule is that the bigger they are, the milder their flavour. Small chillies are therefore the hottest, their fire originating from their seeds and white pith. Chillies are very frequently, though sparingly, used in Indian curries to give a hot flavour. In this book, we mainly use small green finger chillies (hari mirch), which are are unripened red cayenne chillies. Our guide for using these chillies is 1 = mild, 2 = medium, 3 = hot and 4 = very hot. Store fresh chillies in the fridge for 1–2 weeks.

Cloves (laung): these are the dried flower buds of a tree native to the spice islands in Indonesia. They are sweet-scented and used whole in Indian tea (chai), rice dishes, vegetable curries, pickles and mixed masala spices.

Coriander/cilantro (dhainya): can be bought as fresh leaves, whole round seeds and ground into powder. The whole seeds can be dry roasted at the beginning of making a curry dish. Ground coriander is a key ingredient in curry powders, curry pastes and masala mixes. The seeds and powder can be kept for up to 6 months in a cool, dry place. Coriander is related to the parsley and carrot family and the fresh leaves are typically used to complete or garnish a dish, imparting a sweet, citrussy taste and fragrance.

Cumin seeds (jeera): these aromatic, nutty-flavoured, browny-yellow seeds are obtained from a herbaceous plant of the parsley family. They are used to add a mild, sweet aromatic flavour to curries and accompaniments such as pickles and yoghurt dishes, and are often added to breads. The seeds can be bought and used as they are or dry-roasted for an enhanced and stronger flavour. Ground cumin is also available and it, or the crushed seeds, are an important ingredient in curry powder and garam masala.

Curry leaves (kari patta): the fresh and dried leaves are used to impart a mild curry flavour, especially to fish and vegetable dishes.

Curry pastes: these are used to flavour curries. They also add colour; tandoori paste, for instance, reddens a curry, while Madras curry masala imparts a yellow colour. You can make curry pastes yourself but they can also be bought as prepacked blends of spices ground in oil. They are usually quite concentrated and only small amounts need be used to rub into meats or add to marinades or curries. Prepacked varieties can be kept for up to 6 months in a cool, dark place: fresh pastes should be used within 1 week.

Curry powder: a British invention. Curry powder is a blend of several whole spices ground up, often turmeric, coriander/cilantro, mustard seeds, pepper, cumin, ginger and fenugreek, sometimes with cayenne added for heat. It is used as a general substitute for individual spices to impart a curry flavour to food.

Fennel (saunf): fennel has a warm and sweet smell and an anise-type flavour. The greenish-brown seeds are derived from a member of the parsley family. The seeds are popularly used to make tea (chai), are used in some masala blends, and can also be bought sugar-coated to serve at the end of an Indian meal to freshen the breath.

Fenugreek leaves (methi): funugreek leaves are highly pungent and tangy. If bought fresh, the stalks can be snipped and used in addition to the chopped leaves. It is used to make the popular fenugreek cornmeal flat bread (methi di roti) but is also used to flavour other Punjabi breakfast breads such as fried flat breads (parathas). Fenugreek makes a good substitute for coriander/cilantro in most curry dishes, but its flavour is stronger so you may need to use less. The fresh leaves can be stored in the fridge for a few days, and they can also be frozen or dried and stored in an airtight container.

Garam masala: the literal translation is 'hot spices'. Garam masala is brown in colour and is a blend of mild and fragrant spices such as cumin, peppercorns, ginger, cinnamon, cardamom, bay leaves, coriander/cilantro seeds and cloves, but excluding turmeric and chilli powder. It is usually added to curries to finish off the dish and, in the case of wet curries, to thicken the sauce. Garam masala can be made at home (see page 15), or bought as prepacked whole spices and roasted to enhance the flavour, then ground in a coffee grinder or using a pestle and mortar, or bought ready ground in small containers. Store in an airtight container for up to 6 months.

Green cardamom (hari elachi): these small green pods are derived from a perennial plant related to the ginger family. Their warm and pungent, slightly lemon-and-eucalyptus flavour is much milder than brown cardamoms. They are bought whole as unsplit pods or as ground powder. Whole pods can be split before using to release the seeds and give a stronger flavour. Green cardamom is used to lightly fragrant both sweet and savoury Indian dishes, from curries and garam masala to Indian tea (chai) and desserts. The seeds can also be chewed to sweeten the breath. Keep in an airtight container and store in a cool, dark place.

Lovage/carom seeds (ajowain): similar to cumin seeds but a lot spicier. They are used to flavour Punjabi pastries and snacks and Bombay mix.

Mint (pudina): used mainly to flavour chutneys and yoghurt. Can also be added to some desserts and drinks. Buy fresh or bottled.

Mustard seeds (rai): small round, pungent, slightly bitter seeds. They come in white, honey-coloured and black varieties, black being most popular. Used to flavour curries.

Onion seeds/nigella (kalonjii): black, sharp-edged seeds of a herbaceous flower of the buttercup family, with an oregano-like taste. Can be dry-roasted to release the flavour or added to the butter or oil seasoning (tharka) in vegetable and dhal dishes. Also great scattered on naans.

Paprika (deghi mirch): derived from pimiento red peppers. Paprika is used to impart a red colour in Indian dishes and can be rubbed into meats and vegetables to add a mildly aromatic sweet flavour or sprinkled on to accompaniments such as yoghurt. It is an essential ingredient of tandoori masala. Buy in a small container and store in a cool, dark place for up 4 months.

Red chilli (lal mirch): ripened red chillis called cayenne chillis. They are used in their fresh and powdered forms to impart the hotness in curries. An uncomfortably hot dish can be cooled by stirring in yoghurt, by adding a slice of lemon or lime or some juice, a pinch of sugar, or a little tomato sauce.

Rose water (gulab jal): used to impart a rose flavour to sweet Indian dishes such as gulab jaman and rice pudding (kheer). In Indian food stores it can be found in a 1 in 40 dilution of concentrated essence extracted straight from rose petals.

Saffron: saffron is the dried stigmas of the bright purple Crocus sativus flower. It's sometimes called 'the king of spices' and is certainly very expensive. It is used in very small amounts to impart a bright yellow colour and delicate honey flavour to Indian vegetable, meat, rice and sweet dishes. You buy it as threads to crush and add to a dish or to steep in a few tablespoonfuls of hot water or another liquid within the dish. For rice dishes the threads can be added directly to the rice while cooking.

Tamarind (imli): the pulp of the dark brown tamarind fruit pod is compressed, dried and concentrated into a sticky block. The bought block is soaked in water and sieved before use. It can also be bought in liquid form. Tamarind has a distinctive tangy sweet-and-sour flavour similar to, say, sour prunes and is therefore used in chutneys, the classic Punjabi chutney being imli ki.

Tandoori masala: a blend of strongly aromatic ground spices used to impart flavour and a red colour to Indian curries. The blend usually comprises ground paprika, cumin, black pepper, ginger, garlic, bay leaves, cinnamon, cloves, fenugreek, coriander/cilantro and cardamom, with cayenne to make it slightly hot in flavour. Tandoori masala is used in marinades and can be rubbed directly on to meats. Store in dark containers for up to 6 months. See our recipe for home-made tandoori masala on page 15.

Turmeric (haldi): turmeric is a plant root ground and sold in powdered form. It gives the characteristic yellow/orange colour to Indian curries and is an essential ingredient in curry powder. It is has a warm, mild flavour when used in small amounts, but be careful as too much turmeric can impart a bitter taste. Turmeric also has antiseptic properties. Store in a cool, dark place.

Other general spices/blends: black pepper (kali mirch); chana masala – a blend of zingy spices containing coriander/cilantro, cumin, chillies, pomegranate, mango, cloves, black cardamom, cinnamon, black pepper, bay leaves and salt to add to chick pea/garbanzo dishes; chicken masala – a blend of coriander, chillies, cumin, turmeric, fenugreek, ginger, bay leaf, cinnamon, cardamom and paprika; garlic (lasan), ginger (adrak); salt (namak); Indian whole pickling spice (panch puran) – a mixture of whole fennel, mustard, fenugreek, cumin and black onion seeds.

Well-known Indian Food Terms

Balti: a restaurant-coined term which literally translated means 'bucket'. Balti dishes are usually cooked slowly in a cast iron bucket or wok-like dish, then served in smaller balti dishes usually made of steel.

Bhartha: meaning 'mashed mixture', this is usually vegetables, such as aubergine/eggplant (bengan) that have been roughly mashed.

Bhuna: means 'roasted'. A popular example is bhuna bengan bhartha.

Bhurji: 'scrambled' vegetables.

Biryani: a one-pan dish of rice cooked with spiced-up meat or vegetables.

Chaat masala: chaat is a tangy sweet or savoury snack often sold by street sellers. The sweet version is usually a mixture of several Indian fruits sprinkled with fruit chaat masala comprising mango (aamchur) powder, pomegranate (anardana) powder and cinnamon (dalchini). A savoury chaat masala can be made from ground black peppercorns (kali mirch), cumin (jeera), lovage/carom (ajowain) seeds, pomegranate powder, mango powder, asafoetida, cayenne pepper (lal mirch), ground coriander/cilantro (dhainya) and bay leaves (tejpat). It is added to a savoury dish with yoghurt and tamarind (imli) chutney to give a tangy snack. Both types of chaat masala can be bought as prepacked prepared blends.

Curry: a British term to describe any savoury Indian dish containing spices.

Jalfrezi: a restaurant-coined term that refers to a quick stir-fry dish with hot green chillies, green peppers and onions.

Karahi: a large, rounded Indian wok-like utensil used in the home to fry/sauté snacks or to cook thick/dry meat dishes. Karahis come in different sizes and can also be used to serve curries.

Korma: a restaurant-coined term used to describe a mild rather than spicy chicken or vegetable dish cooked in a yoghurt or cream sauce, flavoured with fragrant spices such as cardamom, coriander/cilantro and tumeric.

Makhani murgi: a Punjabi term to describe chicken cooked in butter or ghee flavoured with spices.

Pilau: a restaurant term for mildly spiced rice, usually coloured yellow, orange or red, with a few vegetables.

Sabji: dry vegetable dishes.

Tandoori: this is a name for foods cooked in a earthern 'tandoor' oven, with a fierce coal fire that cooks the food quickly to give a crisp outside and moist inside. Rotis, naans and marinated meats, fish and paneer can all be cooked in this way.

Thali: this is an entire meal served in individual dishes presented on a silver platter. A vegetarian thali might comprise dhal, sabji, yoghurt, pickle, roti, rice and dessert: a mixed meat and vegetarian thali would have all of the above plus a meat curry.

Thari: this means 'sauce', so it can refer to any dish made in a sauce.

Tharka: fried/sautéed seasoning added to the end of a dhal to finish it off. In some parts of India, onions and garlic is not eaten, so the tharka comprises fried spices in oil or clarified butter (ghee). In other parts of India, such as the northern regions, the tharka traditionally includes onion, garlic and ginger. Our Punjabi dhals are based on this latter type.

Tikka: a blend of ground spices used to impart a golden-yellow colour.

Home-made Masalas
and Paneer

You can always use ready-made masalas and spice blends as there are plenty of excellent-quality products on the market. If you do have a little more time, however, it is very satisfying to make your own. Here are our family recipes.

TANDOORI PASTE

5 garlic cloves

10 cm/4 in piece of root ginger

1–2 green chillies, according to taste

3 green cardamom pods

$\frac{1}{2}$ tsp cumin seeds

juice of $\frac{1}{2}$ lemon

1 tsp garam masala (see opposite)

1 tsp paprika

1 tsp freshly ground black pepper

1 tsp turmeric

1 Whiz together the garlic, ginger, chillis, whole cardamom pods, cumin seeds and lemon juice in a grinder until well blended.

2 Turn into a large mixing bowl, add the remaining spices and mix well to an even, paste-like texture.

3 Cover with clingfilm (plastic wrap) and store in the fridge. Use within 1 week.

TIKKA PASTE

1 tsp garlic paste

2 tsp ginger paste

1–2 green chillies, according to taste

1 tsp garam masala (see opposite)

$\frac{3}{4}$ tsp ground coriander (cilantro)

$\frac{3}{4}$ tsp ground cumin

$\frac{3}{4}$ tsp medium curry powder

2 tbsp oil

juice of $\frac{1}{2}$ lemon

1 Blend together all the ingredients in a mixing bowl.

2 Add to any curry dish or marinade or rub straight into meats.

3 Cover any left over and keep in an airtight container in the fridge. Use within 1 week.

TANDOORI MASALA

8 tbsp coriander (cilantro) seeds

4 tsp black peppercorns

8 tbsp cumin seeds

4 tbsp cloves

8 bay leaves

seeds from 24 brown cardamom pods

12 x 4 cm/1¹/₂ in cinnamon sticks

8 tbsp paprika

2 tsp cayenne

3 tbsp fenugreek leaves

4 tbsp garlic powder

4 tbsp ground ginger

1 Whiz together all the spices in a grinder until well blended.

2 Store in an airtight container for up to 6 months.

GARAM MASALA

8 tbsp coriander (cilantro) seeds

4 tsp black peppercorns

8 tbsp cumin seeds

4 tbsp cloves

8 bay leaves

24 brown cardamom pods

12 x 4 cm/1¹/₂ in cinnamon sticks

1 Whiz together all the spices in a grinder until well blended.

2 Store in an airtight container for up to 6 months.

FRESH HOME-MADE PANEER

Paneer, commonly described as Indian cheese, is wholesome, nutritious and rich in protein. It is basically whey pieces separated from the watery part of whole milk and has a texture similar to soya bean and a milky taste. Paneer is a great meat substitute and can be used as it is, scrambled or cubed, or popularly fried in hot vegetable oil, which gives it a crunchy bite that's great in curries. Fried paneer cubes can be frozen when cooled. If you haven't got any lemons, you can use bottled lemon juice.

makes about 250 g/9 oz | **preparation 15 minutes** | **cooking 10 minutes**

2.25 litres/4 pts full-fat milk   **2¹/₂ cups vegetable oil**
1 cup vinegar or ¹/₂ cup lemon juice

1   Bring the milk to the boil in a large saucepan over a medium heat.

2   Turn down the heat and, while the milk is simmering, add the lemon juice or vinegar and stir with a wooden spoon. The whey or solids will separate from the water.

3   Strain the paneer in a colander lined with a tea towel (dish cloth) or muslin (cheesecloth). Rinse under cold running water to remove the acid flavour.

4   The paneer can be used as it is ('scrambled') or it can be set as a block.

5   To make a block, lift the paneer out of the colander using the tea towel or muslin. Fold over the ends of the material to cover it completely.

6   Using your hands, squeeze out the excess water and mould and flatten the paneer to form either a round or a rectangular block. Transfer the block in the material to a microwaveable plate.

7   Fill a heavy pan with water and place it on the block. Leave for about 15 minutes to remove more of the water.

8   Lift off the pan and drain the liquid from the plate. Microwave on High for 10 minutes to further set the block.

9   Allow to cool for 5 minutes, then peel off the tea towel. The paneer can be used as it is or cut into 2.5 cm/1 in cubes and deep- or shallow-fried in hot vegetable oil until golden brown.

Tips for Authentic Indian Cooking

- Measurements: most Indian cooks do not use scales so the ingredients are roughly measured using cups and spoons. Dishes are seasoned and ingredients modified according to individual tastes. So experiment!

- Leftover vegetable and paneer dishes make excellent snacks for lunch or brunch when stuffed into hot pittas and served with chutney, pickles etc.

- Garlic cloves are easy to peel if soaked in a little water.

- If you've added too much chilli and your dish is over-hot, add some fresh tomato or tomato sauce, or some lemon or lime juice, or some yoghurt, or a pinch of sugar to make it milder.

- If your dish seems too salty, add a small peeled and grated potato while cooking.

- Recycle: when making paneer from fresh, do not discard the whey water but use it when making roti, pooris or naans. They will turn out softer and tastier.

- To get rid of the smell of garlic on your hands, rub a small amount of coffee or lemon juice into them before washing with soap.

- Grind spices in a coffee grinder and store in an airtight container for up to 6 months. Grind some rice afterwards and discard to remove the spice flavour from the grinder.

- Rice: undercook slightly and let it finish off by itself in its own steam to make it light and fluffy. Add a few lemon drops or a little butter to keep plain rice grains separate.

- Thickening: curry sauce can be thickened by adding the garam masala at the end, or a small peeled and grated potato, or cornflour (cornstarch) mixed to a smooth paste in water. Alternatively, simply remove the lid and simmer the dish for a bit longer.

- Garlic, chillies and ginger can all be crushed/chopped and frozen in ice cube trays, or bought as a paste or powder.

- Coriander (cilantro): if using fresh, cut off the ends (about 5 cm/2 in) and discard. Chop finely and freeze in ice cube trays or in small plastic bags. Can also be bought as seeds or powder and paste. Can be substituted for fenugreek leaves.

- Plain parathas and naans can be stuffed with ingredients according to individual taste.

- Okra (ladies' fingers) need first to be washed while whole, then thoroughly dried with a tea towel (dish cloth) or they will exude a sticky substance and become slimy when cooked. To keep okra firm and crunchy, add the salt at the end once the dish has been cooked.

- Whole spices keep for longer than ground.

- Tea spices can be roughly ground using a pestle and mortar or ground in a coffee grinder. They can be stored in an airtight container up to 6 months.

Notes on the Recipes

- For speed and ease, nearly all the ingredients are given in easy measures – spoons, cups, packets and so on – so you don't need measuring scales.

- All spoon measurements are level: 1 tsp = 5 ml; 1 tbsp = 15 ml.

- 1 cup = 250 ml/8 fl oz.

- Ingredients are listed in the order in which they are used in the recipe.

- American terms are given in brackets.

- Always wash, peel, core and seed, if necessary, fresh foods before use. Ensure that all produce is as fresh as possible and in good condition.

- How hot you like your dishes is a matter of personal taste so adjust quantities to make the food how you like it. As a general rule, use one green finger chilli for a mild dish, two for medium, three for hot and four for very hot.

- Use fresh herbs if possible. If you do use dried herbs, use half the quantity. Chopped frozen varieties are much better than dried. There is no substitute for fresh parsley and coriander (cilantro).

- Use canned tomatoes if you don't have fresh.

- Can, pot and packet sizes are approximate and will depend on the brand.

- Use your own discretion in substituting ingredients and personalising the recipes. Make notes of particular successes so you can make them again.

- Use whatever kitchen gadgets you like to speed up preparation and cooking times: a mixer for whisking; a food processor for grating, slicing, mixing or kneading; a blender for liquidising; a coffee grinder for grinding spices.

- All ovens vary, so cooking times are approximate. Adjust cooking times and temperatures according to your manufacturer's instructions.

- Always preheat a conventional oven and cook on the centre shelf unless otherwise specified. Fan ovens do not require preheating.

- As only a little oil is used in our recipes, it is best to use non-stick saucepans or add extra oil, or a few tablespoonfuls of water or half a tomato to dry dishes to prevent them sticking.

Shuratt Ki Cheej

SOMETHING TO START

This chapter contains a selection of delicious appetisers, ranging from light bites to hearty snacks. There is a wide array of Punjabi snacks to choose from, including popular samosas and sizzling kebabs. In Indian households, snacks such as Wadhia Sabji Wale Samosae (Brilliant Vegetable Samosas, see page 24), Etwar Ki Aloo Palak Pakorae (Sunday Afternoon Potato and Spinach Fritters, see page 27), Mummyji's Alaag Aloo Tikkis (Mum's Different Potato Patties, see page 22) and Sabji te Paneer Wale Spring Rolls(Vegetable and Paneer Spring Rolls, see page 32) are conjured up in moments.

Starters are typically served at social occasions from birthdays and weddings to community gatherings and dinner parties, or simply enjoyed on a lazy Sunday afternoon with the family and a hot cup of masala chai. And as well as being served on their own, they are often part of the menu for a dinner party.

Chaat Pata Dahi Pappar Aloo Chat

TANGY YOGHURT, POPPADOM AND POTATO SNACK

A tangy snack with a bite, chaat is usually made of yoghurt, gram flour, crunchy bits such as Bombay mix, and topped with a zingy chutney to make your taste buds tingle. It is served wrapped in pieces of newspaper by street sellers in India. We serve it at dinner parties as a starter or as an anytime snack.

serves 4 | preparation 10 minutes | cooking 5 minutes

2 large potatoes, peeled
2 tbsp cumin seeds
1 tsp garam masala
450 ml/³/₄ pt/large pot of plain yoghurt

2–3 green finger chillies, finely chopped
3 ready-made popadoms, roughly
   crushed, or 6 individual popadoms

1 Boil the potatoes whole for 5–6 minutes in boiling water until slightly softened, then drain.

2 Leave until cool enough to handle, then cut into bite-size chunks and set aside.

3 In a frying pan (skillet), dry roast the cumin seeds with the masala for 1 minute until they begin to pop. Remove from the pan and tip into a serving bowl.

4 Stir in the yoghurt, then the chillies. Add the potatoes.

5 Add the crushed popadoms or place individual popadoms on top and serve.

SERVING SUGGESTIONS AND TIPS

- Serve with with Khatti Mithi Imli Ki Chutney (see page 134).
- As a variation, you can fry (sauté) the potatoes, or cut them into wedges, mix with tandoori masala spice and then bake them.

Mummyji's Alaag Aloo Tikkis
MUM'S DIFFERENT POTATO PATTIES

Aloo tikkis are traditionally heavily coated with a batter made from gram flour, and the results can be a bit stodgy. This is a much lighter version, with the fluffy potato filling lightly coated in cornflour. We think these are delicious hot or cold. Make your own garam masala or use ready-made.

serves 4–6 | preparation 15 minutes | cooking 10 minutes

For the patties
12 new or 4 medium potatoes
1 tsp cumin seeds
1¹/₂ tsp garam masala
1 tsp salt
3 heaped tbsp cornflour (cornstarch)
  or gram flour

2–3 green finger chillies, finely chopped
a large handful of chopped fresh
  coriander (cilantro) or a handful of
  dried fenugreek leaves
For the coating
¹/₂ cup cornflour
¹/₂ cup vegetable oil for shallow-frying

1 To make the patties, microwave the potatoes for 3–5 minutes on High until cooked.

2 Place in a bowl and mash with a potato masher (you can discard the skins if you prefer).

3 Add the cumin seeds, garam masala, salt, cornflour or gram flour, chillies and coriander or fenugreek leaves. Mix with a fork or your hand and lightly knead together to form a large round.

4 With lightly floured hands, take a satsuma-sized piece of the potato filling and flatten it a little. Roll it lightly in the cornflour and set to one side on a plate. Repeat with the remaining mixture.

5 Heat the oil and shallow-fry the aloo tikkis on both sides in batches of four for about 5 minutes until golden brown.

SERVING SUGGESTIONS AND TIPS

- Serve with Dahi Wale Punjabi Chole (see opposite), Pudina Dahi (see page 136) or Khatti Mithi Imli Ki Chutney (see page 134).

- If you are in a hurry, use ordinary ketchup (catsup) as an accompaniment.

- For an extra-crispy texture, deep-fry the aloo tikkis.

Dahi Wale Punjabi Chole

PUNJABI YOGHURT CHICK PEAS

*This is a real Punjabi-style dish — nutty chick peas coated in a blend of zingy spices
and a thick yoghurt sauce. It is a very popular and scrumptious option that is
often served at Indian weddings, special meals and festivals. It is traditionally served
with aloo tikki and samosas.*

serves 4–6 | preparation 10 minutes | cooking 25 minutes

2 tsp cumin seeds

3–4 tbsp olive oil

2 onions, finely chopped

4 cm/1½ in piece of root ginger, grated

4 garlic cloves, crushed

1½ tsp salt

1 tsp turmeric

1¾ tsp tandoori masala

1¾ tsp chana masala

2–3 large tomatoes, chopped

150 ml/¼ pt/small pot of plain yoghurt

400 g/14 oz/large can of chick peas
   (garbanzos), drained and washed

1 cup water

2–3 green finger chillies, finely chopped

1½ tsp garam masala

a large handful of chopped fresh
   coriander (cilantro), to garnish

1 Place the cumin seeds in a saucepan over a medium heat and dry roast for
  1 minute until they pop.

2 Add the oil and heat gently for a minute, then add the onions, ginger and garlic.
  Cook for about 3 minutes until golden brown, stirring frequently.

3 Add the salt, turmeric, tandoori masala and chana masala and stir for 1 minute.

4 Add the tomatoes and yoghurt and cook for about 5 minutes, stirring until a
  smooth paste forms.

5 Add the chick peas and the water and cook for 10–15 minutes until the liquid has
  reduced to one-third.

6 Reduce the heat, stir in the chillies (two for medium or three for hot) and add the
  garam masala.

7 Serve garnished with the coriander.

SERVING SUGGESTIONS AND TIPS

- Serve with Mummyji's Alaag Aloo Tikkis (see opposite), or Wadhia Sabji Wali
  Samosae (see page 24), or Keema Samosae (see page 38) and Khatti Mithi Imli Ki
  Chutney (see page 134) or Masala Dahi (see page 138) as an accompaniment.

Wadhia Sabji Wale Samosae

BRILLIANT VEGETABLE SAMOSAS

We remember from our childhoods our mums and aunties getting together to make samosas on a large scale for grand occasions such as weddings, religious blessings or just dinner parties. Making samosas from scratch can be fun and the end result very satisfying, but our quicker option is to use delicious tortilla wraps.

serves 6–8 | preparation 20 minutes | cooking 10 minutes

3 tbsp plain (all-purpose) flour
9 tbsp water
3 large baking potatoes
2 tbsp cumin seeds
2 tsp coriander (cilantro) seeds
7 tbsp olive oil
1 onion, chopped
$\frac{1}{2}$ cup frozen peas

2 tsp salt
$2\frac{1}{2}$ heaped tsp garam masala
$1\frac{1}{2}$ tsp pomegranate powder (optional)
2–4 green finger chillies, finely chopped
1 packet of 6 or 8 medium-sized tortillas wraps
$2\frac{1}{2}$ cups vegetable oil

1 Mix the flour with the water to make a thick paste. Set aside.

2 Prick the potatoes and microwave on High for 8 minutes until soft. Set aside.

3 In a medium saucepan, dry roast the cumin and coriander seeds over a medium heat for 1 minute until they pop. Add the olive oil, heat, then add the onion and lightly brown for 3–4 minutes. Add the frozen peas and fry (sauté) for a further 2 minutes.

4 Add the salt, garam masala, pomegranate powder, if using, and chillies and mix thoroughly. Switch off the heat.

5 Coarsly mash the potato with a fork or potato masher (you can leave the skin on if you prefer). Add to the pan of spices and mix thoroughly.

6 Halve the tortillas. Take one half and, with the straight edge near you, fold the left side two-thirds over the centre. Brush the top of the folded piece with the paste and fold the other side over it to form a cone. Press together with your fingers to form a firm seal.

7 Fill the cone with the potato mixture. Brush the inner edges with the paste and press the top together firmly with your fingers to seal. Repeat until all the tortilla halves and the potato filling are used.

8 Heat the vegetable oil until hot and shallow-fry the samosas, turning frequently, until evenly cooked, crispy and golden brown.

SERVING SUGGESTIONS AND TIPS

- Serve with Dahi Wale Punjabi Chole (see page 23) for a special occasion or eat hot with Khatti Mithi Imli Ki Chutney (see page 134) or even just good old tomato ketchup (catsup) or brown sauce with a cup of hot Masala Chai (see page 130).

- These samosas are quite large, but they can be cut in half or into bite-sized pieces for a dinner party. Just spear the pieces on to cocktail sticks (toothpicks) or use fingers, Punjabi style.

- You could use filo pastry (paste) instead of tortilla wraps.

- Instead of deep-frying the samosas, you could brush them with vegetable oil and bake them at 180°C/350°F/gas 4/fan oven 160°C for 20 minutes until golden brown. Baking gives a crisper samosa.

Bhuna Kaju te Badam

ROASTED CASHEW NUTS AND ALMONDS

This is a savoury, crunchy, munchy snack that was a real hit with all our family and friends at Babita's brother's wedding celebrations. Snack away with a cold Indian beer or a tall glass of gin and tonic and plenty of light-hearted conversation. It's so easy to make and absolutely delicious.

serves 6–8 | preparation 2 minutes | cooking 15 minutes

3 tbsp olive oil
1¹/₂ cups unsalted whole cashew nuts
1¹/₂ cups unsalted whole almonds

1¹/₂ tsp salt
3 tsp paprika
1 tsp freshly ground black pepper

1 Heat the oil in a large frying pan (skillet) or wok for 1 minute over a medium heat.

2 Add all the nuts and stir-fry for 1 minute, then reduce the heat to low and let the nuts roast for 2 minutes.

3 Add the salt, paprika and pepper and stir thoroughly until the nuts are evenly coated.

4 Leave to cook over a low heat for about 10 minutes, tossing the nuts in the pan so that they don't burn (you want to achieve a roasted effect).

Punjabi Sabji Kebab

PUNJABI VEGETABLE KEBABS

These are delicious kebabs made with succulent fresh vegetables marinated in spicy flavours that race across your palate with a zingy edge. You can use ready-made tandoori masala or, for a more authentic taste, try making your own blend from the recipe on page 15. These kebabs can also be cooked on the barbecue.

serves 4–6 | preparation 10 minutes | marinating 20 minutes | cooking 10 minutes

1 large aubergine (eggplant), sliced into 2 cm/³/₄ in thick rounds
250 g/9 oz whole button mushrooms
10 very small whole roasting onions or shallots
10 cherry tomatoes
1 red (bell) pepper, seeded and cut into squares
1 yellow pepper, seeded and cut into squares

4 red or green jalapeño chillies
1¹/₂ tsp salt
2 tsp paprika
2 tbsp tandoori masala
1 tsp freshly ground black pepper
juice of 2 limes
6 tbsp olive oil
a handful of chopped fresh coriander (cilantro), to garnish

1 Place the aubergine, mushrooms, onions or shallots, tomatoes and peppers in a mixing bowl.

2 Halve the chillies lengthways and add the flesh and seeds to the vegetables.

3 Add the salt, paprika, tandoori masala, pepper and lime juice. Add the oil and toss thoroughly. Cover with clingfilm (plastic wrap) and chill for at least 20 minutes or until ready to cook.

4 Gently thread the vegetable pieces alternately on to metal or soaked wooden skewers.

5 Cook the kebabs under a hot grill (broiler) for 7–10 minutes, turning constantly and brushing with the remaining marinade.

6 Serve garnished with the coriander.

SERVING SUGGESTIONS AND TIPS

- Serve with Dahi te Dudh Wale Sada Naan (see page 103), pitta bread or tortilla wraps and a mixed green salad and lemon wedges.

Etwar Ki Aloo Palak Pakorae

SUNDAY AFTERNOON POTATO AND SPINACH FRITTERS

A firm Punjabi household favourite, there is nothing like the taste of these mouth-watering pakorae complemented with a cup of hot, spicy masala chai on a lazy Sunday afternoon. Just add family and friends! A quick dish to show off your culinary skills, these crispy yet succulent golden fritters are absolutely sublime.

serves 6–8 | preparation 10 minutes | cooking 10 minutes

1 cup chick pea (garbanzo) flour
1 large potato, peeled and thinly sliced
1/4 bag baby spinach, roughly chopped
1 onion, finely sliced lengthways
2–3 green finger chillies, finely chopped
1 tbsp cumin seeds
3/4 tsp salt
1 tbsp garam masala

a large handful of fresh coriander (cilantro), chopped
a handful of fresh or 3 tbsp dried fenugreek leaves (optional)
150 ml/1/4 pt/small pot of plain yoghurt
1/4 cup water
2 1/2 cups vegetable oil

1 Sieve the flour into a mixing bowl.

2 Mix in all the remaining ingredients except the water and oil.

3 Add the water a little at a time to form a thick but runny consistency, mixing well with one hand.

4 Heat the oil in a wok until hot. Drop tablespoonfuls of the mixture into the oil and cook in batches of 5–6, stirring occasionally to keep them separate and evenly browned.

5 Drain on kitchen paper (paper towels).

SERVING SUGGESTIONS AND TIPS

- Enjoy with Mr T's Tazhee Pudina Chutney (see page 133), Masala Dahi (see page 138), or just tomato ketchup (catsup), brown sauce or Khatti Mithi Imli Ki Chutney (see page 134) and hot Masala Chai (see page 130).

- As a variation, substitute grated or thinly sliced cauliflower and/or thinly sliced aubergine (eggplant) for the spinach.

SOMETHING TO START

Bharmi Shimla Mirch te Tomater

STUFFED PEPPERS AND TOMATOES

*Being vegetarian, our mums are constantly finding new ways to stuff vegetables.
These peppers and tomatoes are a fusion of bright colours and spices that liven up
simple quick masala mashed potatoes. We like to use the microwave whenever we
can because it saves so much time.*

serves 4 | preparation 15 minutes | cooking 30 minutes

2 large baking potatoes
4 large fresh tomatoes
4 (bell) peppers (any colour or mixed)
2 tbsp cumin seeds
4 tbsp olive oil, plus extra for greasing
   and drizzling
1 large onion, chopped
3 garlic cloves, crushed

4 cm/1½ in piece of root ginger, grated
1 tsp turmeric
¾ tbsp garam masala
1 tsp salt
2–3 green finger chillies, finely chopped
a large handful of fresh coriander
   (cilantro), chopped

1 Preheat the oven to 180°C/350°F/gas 4/fan oven 160°C.

2 Prick the potatoes with a fork and microwave on High for 10-12 minutes. Allow to
cool for 2 minutes.

3 Slice off the tops of the tomatoes and peppers and reserve. Scrape the seeds out
of the peppers and discard.

4 In a frying pan (skillet), dry-roast the cumin seeds over a medium heat for
1 minute. Add the oil, onion, garlic and ginger and fry (sauté) for 3 minutes,
stirring frequently, until lightly browned.

5 Add the turmeric, garam masala, salt and chillies. Fry for a further 2 minutes to
cook the spices, then remove from the heat.

6 Slice in the potatoes in half. Using a spoon, scoop out the insides and add to the
onion mixture (the skins can be added or discarded). Mash roughly with a fork.
Scoop out the tomato pulps and add to the pan. Add the coriander and mix
roughly.

7 Stuff each tomato and pepper with the spicy potato mixture and cover with the
'lids'. Place on a lightly oiled baking (cookie) sheet, drizzle lightly with oil and
bake for 30 minutes until golden brown.

- Serve with just salad or as part of a main meal with rice, salad and yoghurt and an extra curry of your choice.

- As a variation, peel the uncooked potatoes and cut into bite-size chunks. Parboil over a medium heat for 5 minutes. Drain, then fry with the onion, garlic and ginger until lightly browned. Add the spices and cook for about 5 minutes until the potatoes are golden brown. Add the tomato pulp and fry all together for 1–2 minutes. Remove from the heat and add the coriander. When cool, stuff the peppers and tomatoes and bake as above.

Sona's Desi Salad

SONA'S INDIAN SALAD

This is Babita's mum's recipe for a multi-purpose salad-with-a-difference that can be enjoyed by itself or used to complement just about any Indian curry dish. The ginger and lime really adds an exciting kick and sets your taste buds buzzing. Add the chillies if you dare!

serves 4–6 | preparation 10 minutes

2 large carrots
1 large cucumber
5 cm/2 in piece of root ginger
1 large red onion, thinly sliced
³/₄ tsp salt
³/₄ tsp freshly ground black pepper
1 tbsp olive oil

juice of 1 lemon
juice of 1 lime
a handful of fresh coriander (cilantro), chopped
2 small green finger chillies, thinly sliced (optional)

1 Thinly slice the carrots and cucumber into 4 cm/1¹/₂ in strips. Cut the ginger into long, very thin strips. Thoroughly wash all of the salad ingredients with cold water and pat dry.

2 Place the carrot, cucumber, ginger and onion slices in a large salad bowl and add the salt, pepper, oil and lemon and lime juice. Toss in the coriander and chillies, if using.

3 Mix together thoroughly to coat the salad in the dressing.

Desi Paneer Tikka

INDIAN CHEESY BITES

These are a tasty milky, spongy and spicy filling snack, often served at Indian weddings or special occasions. They are best eaten with your fingers and dipped into chilli sauce. You can use ready-made tikka paste and paneer from a supermarket or Indian store, or make your own for a really authentic flavour.

serves 4–6 | **preparation 10 minutes** | **marinating 20 minutes** | **cooking 10 minutes**

3 garlic cloves
5 cm/2 in piece of root ginger
3 green finger chillies
2 tbsp olive oil
juice of 1 lemon
400 g/14 oz bought or home-made
   paneer, chopped into 4 cm/1½ in cubes

1½ tsp salt
2 tbsp tikka paste
150 ml/¼ pt/small pot of Greek yoghurt
1 onion, thinly sliced
a handful of fresh chopped coriander
   (cilantro), to garnish

1 Whiz together the garlic, ginger, chillies, half the oil and the lemon juice in a blender or grinder to form a smooth paste. Add 1 tbsp of water, if necessary, to help blend the ingredients together. Pour into a mixing bowl.

2 Add the paneer cubes, the salt, tikka paste and yoghurt.

3 Mix well, cover with clingfilm (plastic wrap) and chill for at least 20 minutes or until ready to cook.

4 Gently thread the paneer cubes on to metal or soaked wooden skewers. Grill (broil) under a medium heat for 8–10 minutes, turning and basting, until the paneer is golden brown.

5 Meanwhile, heat the remaining oil in a frying pan (skillet) for 1 minute, then add the onion and cook for about 3 minutes until golden brown.

6 Transfer to a serving dish, then place the grilled paneer tikka on top of the onions and garnish with the coriander before serving.

SERVING SUGGESTIONS AND TIPS

- Enjoy with mixed shredded salad, lemon wedges and Mr T's Tazhee Pudina Chutney (see page 133).

Ajowain Mattarey

CAROM FINGER BISCUITS

If you like savoury snacks with your tea then this recipe is for you. Golden finger biscuits flavoured with carom seeds for a mild spicy flavour – delicious and a firm Punjabi favourite. These are popularly served with Masala Chai (see page 130) for family and friends.

serves 4 | preparation 15 minutes | cooking 10 minutes

1 cup plain flour
$^3/_4$ tsp salt
$^1/_4$ tsp carom seeds
$^1/_4$ tsp black pepper

2$^1/_4$ cups vegetable oil
$^1/_4$ cup water
2 cups vegetable oil

1 Place the flour, salt, carom seeds and black pepper in a shallow dish or mixing bowl.

2 Add $^1/_4$ cup of the vegetable oil a little at a time and mix in well by hand or using a spatula. Add the water a little at a time and mix to form a dough. Leave to rest for 10 minutes.

3 Knead the dough briefly, then roll out on a floured board. Cut into thin strips about 1 cm/$^1/_2$ in wide and 10 cm/4 in long with a knife.

4 Heat the remaining oil and deep-fry the dough strips until golden brown. Drain on kitchen paper (paper towels) and serve hot.

5 Any remainders can be stored in an airtight container. Eat within a month.

SERVING SUGGESTIONS AND TIPS

- As a variation, cut the dough into rounds instead of strips to make Mathhian.

Sabji te Paneer Wale Spring Rolls

VEGETABLE AND PANEER SPRING ROLLS

Spring rolls Indian-style are extremely popular vegetarian snacks at weddings and in Indian households for guests and dinner parties. Usually the pastry is made from scratch from flour and water but our inventive short cut uses delicious tortilla wraps to get the same effect – plus the spring rolls are much bigger!

serves 6–8 | preparation 20 minutes | cooking 10 minutes

3 tbsp plain (all-purpose) flour
9 tbsp water
2 large carrots, grated
½ cup frozen sweetcorn (corn)
2–3 green finger chillies, finely chopped
1 tsp salt

2 tsp garam masala
1 cup scrambled paneer (see page 16)
1 packet of 6 or 8 medium-sized tortilla
 wraps
7–10 tbsp olive oil

1 Mix the flour with the water to make a thick paste. Set aside.

2 Place the carrots, sweetcorn, chillies, salt, garam masala and paneer in a mixing bowl and combine with a fork.

3 Halve the tortillas. Place 3 tablespoonfuls of the vegetable mixture in the centre of one half and distribute it lengthways.

4 Fold in the ends first, then roll lengthways. Brush with the flour paste and press firmly together with your fingers.

5 Heat the oil until hot and shallow-fry the rolls until crispy and golden brown.

SERVING SUGGESTIONS AND TIPS

- Serve with Khatti Mithi Imli Ki Chutney (see page 134) or just tomato ketchup (catsup) or brown sauce, with a cup of hot Masala Chai (see page 130).

- These are quite large, but they can be cut in half or into bite-sized pieces for a dinner party. Just spear the pieces on to cocktail sticks (toothpicks) or use fingers, Punjabi style.

- You could use filo pastry (paste) or spring roll pastry instead of tortilla wraps.

- Instead of deep-frying the spring rolls, you could brush them with vegetable oil and bake them at 180°C/350°F/gas 4/fan oven 160°C for 20 minutes until golden brown. Baking gives a crisper spring roll.

Mirchi Shaley

PAPRIKA CORN ON THE COB

The combination of red chilli powder, paprika and lemon and lime juice in this dish is sensational – it makes the corn so lip-smackingly delicious that you can't stop nibbling at it. This is often served at outdoor summer meals and festivals, but you don't have to wait for an excuse like that to try it.

serves 4–6 | preparation 5 minutes | marinating 10 minutes | cooking 15 minutes

6 large corn cobs
3 tbsp olive oil
1¹/₂ tsp salt
4 tsp paprika

1 tsp chilli powder
juice of 2 lemons
juice of 2 limes

1 Preheat the oven to 180°C/350°F/gas 4/fan oven 160°C.

2 Boil the corn cobs in a large pan of water for about 5 minutes until they begin to soften and are partly cooked.

3 Mix together the oil, salt, paprika, chilli powder and lemon and lime juice in a large bowl.

4 Immerse the corn cobs in the oil mixture, cover the bowl with clingfilm (plastic wrap) and leave to marinate for at least 10 minutes or until ready to cook.

5 Wrap each of the cobs individually in foil, place on a baking (cookie) sheet and cook on the top oven shelf for 8–10 minutes.

SERVING SUGGESTIONS AND TIPS

- These are great to serve for party food and are perfect for summer barbecues.

- You can snap a cob in half if you prefer smaller corn cobs. Remember to do this before you start cooking in the oven, and use the minimum cooking time given.

- For a more authentic taste, instead of oven-baking the cobs try toasting them on a barbecue or even a gas hob.

Swadish Salmon Ki Tikki

TASTY SALMON BITES

Try these melt-in-the-mouth, ever-so-light fish bites with a zingy lime, paprika and chilli kick. You can replace the salmon fillets with any firm white fish. The three green finger chillies we recommend here will give you a hot dish, but you can always use fewer if you prefer. A great recipe for special occasions!

serves 4–6 | preparation 10 minutes | cooking 10 minutes

1 onion, roughly chopped
7.5 cm/3 in piece of root ginger
3 green finger chillies, chopped
6 tbsp olive oil
juice of 2 limes
1 egg
4 square wheat crackers
$^1\!/_2$ tsp salt

1$^1\!/_2$ tsp paprika
1 tsp cumin seeds
4 salmon fillets (about 400 g/14 oz), roughly cut into 1 cm/$^1\!/_2$ in cubes
a large handful of fresh coriander (cilantro), finely chopped
2 tbsp cornflour (cornstarch)
lemon wedges, to garnish

1 Using a blender, whiz together the onion, ginger, chillies, 1 tbsp of the oil, the lime juice, egg, crackers, salt, paprika and cumin.

2 Pour into a mixing bowl and add the salmon cubes and coriander. Mix well by hand or with a fork.

3 Take a golf-ball-sized portion of the fish mixture, roll it into a ball and pat flat into a round about 1–2 cm/$^1\!/_2$–$^3\!/_4$ in thick. Lightly roll in the cornflour and set aside on a plate. Repeat with the remaining fish mixture.

4 Heat the remaining oil in a frying pan (skillet) over a medium to high heat for about 2 minutes. Fry (sauté) the rounds in batches of four for about 3–5 minutes on each side until golden brown.

5 Garnish with lemon wedges and serve.

SERVING SUGGESTIONS AND TIPS

• The smaller you make the fish patties, the easier they are to cook without breaking up.

• If your mixture is too wet, coat with more cornflour before frying.

Machchi Tikka

FISH TIKKA

This is a quick, easy-to-make and very tasty tikka masala dish. The results are lightly crusted edges on the outside with tender moist fish inside and loads of flavour. You can use any white fish – cod or monkfish is a good choice. For a more authentic taste try making your own tikka paste (see page 14).

serves 4–6 | preparation 5 minutes | marinating 30 minutes | cooking 15 minutes

4 skinless white fish fillets
  (about 400–600 g/14 oz–1 lb 6 oz)
2 tbsp tikka paste
3 tbsp Greek yoghurt
½ tsp salt
2 bay leaves

2 tbsp olive oil
1 lemon, sliced
a handful of salad and a handful of
  chopped fresh coriander (cilantro),
  to garnish

1 Cut the fillets into strips about 10 cm/4 in long.

2 Mix the tikka paste with the yoghurt and salt in a bowl and add the bay leaves.

3 Add the fish strips to the bowl, cover with clingfilm (plastic wrap) and leave to marinade in the fridge for at least 30 minutes or until ready to cook.

4 Pre-heat the oven to 180°C/350°F/gas 4/fan oven 160°C.

5 Brush a baking (cookie) sheet with the oil.

6 Place the marinated fish strips on the baking tray and bake on the top oven shelf for about 6–7 minutes, then turn over and bake for a further 6–7 minutes.

7 Garnish with the lemon slices, salad and coriander and serve.

SERVING SUGGESTIONS AND TIPS

- Enjoy with Pudina Dahi (see page 136).

- The fish can also be barbecued or chargrilled instead of baking in the oven.

- A quick way of testing how fish is cooked. Using a fork press down on the fish: if it bouncy then it's 'medium' cooked; if it oozes juice then it's 'rare' cooked; if it is hard and there is no movement then it's 'well' cooked.

Tandoori Shahi Jhinga

TANDOORI KING PRAWNS

This dish tastes wicked, looks sensational and is so simple to cook. Giant king prawns are covered in smooth creamy yoghurt and flavoured with delicate tandoori spices – the longer you leave the prawns to marinate the more potent the flavours will be.

serves 4–6 | preparation 15 minutes | marinating 30 minutes | cooking 10 minutes

20 raw unpeeled king tiger prawns
   (shrimp)
juice of 1 lemon
juice of 1 lime
$1/4$ tsp salt
$1/2$ tsp freshly ground black pepper

2 tbsp tandoori paste
150 ml/$1/4$ pt/small pot of Greek yoghurt
lemon slices, lime slices and a handful of
   chopped fresh coriander (cilantro),
   to garnish

1 Peel the prawns. Cut down the middle to expose and remove the black vein. Rinse the prawns in cold running water.

2 Mix together the lemon and lime juice, the salt and pepper. Add the prawns and leave for 5 minutes to soak up all the juices.

3 Blend together the tandoori paste and yoghurt until evenly pink.

4 Add the tandoori paste mixture to the prawns and mix well. Cover with clingfilm (plastic wrap) and leave to marinate in the fridge for at least 30 minutes or until ready to cook.

5 Cook the prawns on the barbecue or under a preheated grill (broiler). They will need only about 2 minutes on each side.

6 Garnish with lemon and lime slices and the coriander and serve.

SERVING SUGGESTIONS AND TIPS

• Enjoy with a mixed shredded salad and Piyaz, Tomater te Hari Mirch (see page 135).

Murgi Tikka Tookrae

CHICKEN TIKKA PIECES

In India, chicken is served as a treat and on special occasions. In this recipe, delicate pieces of boneless chicken are marinated in creamy yoghurt enhanced by tikka masala spices. For a more authentic taste, try making your own tikka paste (see page 14). Three chillies gives a hot dish.

serves 4–6 | preparation 10 minutes | marinating 30 minutes | cooking 25 minutes

5 tbsp plain yoghurt
1 tsp salt
2 tbsp tikka paste
4 skinless chicken breasts, diced

2 tbsp olive oil
a large handful of fresh coriander
   (cilantro), chopped
1 lemon or lime, sliced

1 Preheat the oven to 180°C/350°F/gas 4/fan oven 160°C.

2 Mix together the yoghurt, salt and tikka paste. Mix in the chicken and chill for 30 minutes. Brush a baking (cookie) sheet lightly with the oil.

3 Using tongs, remove the chicken from the marinade and place on the baking sheet. Cook in the preheated oven for about 25 minutes, turning occasionally and basting with the remaining marinade.

4 Garnish with the coriander and lemon or lime slices and serve.

SERVING SUGGESTIONS AND TIPS

- Enjoy this dish as a snack with Pudina Dahi (see page 136) or with rice, Tarwala Dahi (see page 136) and fresh roti.

- The chicken can also be cut into larger pieces and barbecued on skewers or chargrilled.

Keema Samosae

MINCED LAMB SAMOSAS

Heavenly, crispy, meaty samosas! Yes, you can buy them ready-made – but home-made tastes so much better. For ease, our recipe skips making the traditional flour and water pastry and instead uses quick tortilla wraps and bakes rather than fries for a lower-fat option. Two chillies make the samosas medium-hot.

makes 6–8 | preparation 20 minutes | cooking 10 minutes

400–600 g/14 oz–1 lb 6 oz lamb mince
2 tsp cumin seeds
2 tsp coriander (cilantro) seeds
5 tbsp olive or vegetable oil, plus extra for brushing
1 onion, chopped
1¼ tbsp salt
1½ tsp garam masala

2–3 green finger chillies, finely chopped
1 tsp pomegranate powder (optional)
1 cup frozen peas
For the flour paste
3 tbsp plain (all-purpose) flour
9 tbsp water
6 or 8 medium-sized tortilla wraps

1 Preheat the oven to 180°C/350°F/gas 4/fan oven 160°C.

2 Fry (sauté) the mince in a large saucepan over a medium heat until brown and the grains are separate. Drain away the excess oil and transfer the mince to a plate.

3 Add the cumin and coriander seeds to the saucepan and roast for 1 minute until they begin to pop. Add the oil and onion and lightly brown for 3 minutes.

4 Add the salt, garam masala, chillies, pomegranate powder, if using, and peas and fry for a further 1 minute. Remove the pan from the heat and set aside.

5 Mix together the flour and water to make a thick paste.

6 Cut the tortillas in half. Take one half and, with the straight edge near you, fold the left side two-thirds over the centre. Brush the top of the folded piece with the paste and fold the other side over it to form a cone. Press together with your fingers to form a firm seal.

7 Fill the cone with the keema mixture. Brush the inner edges with the paste and seal firmly with your fingers. Repeat until all the wraps and filling are used.

8 Brush the samosas with oil, arrange them on a baking (cookie) sheet and bake for 20 minutes until crispy and golden brown.

- Serve with Khatti Mithi Imli Ki Chutney (see page 134) or ordinary tomato ketchup (catsup).
- As a variation, use chicken pieces or minced (ground) chicken instead of the lamb for the filling and follow the same method.
- For a crisper version, you can use filo pastry (paste).
- For a softer texture, shallow-fry the samosas instead of baking them.

Punjabi Seekh Kebab

PUNJABI MINCE KEBABS

Luscious velvety lamb mince kebabs spiced with garlic, ginger and tandoori spices, Punjabi style. These are delicious served as a snack or as part of a main meal in hot wraps or naans. They are really easy to make. Two chillies makes for a medium dish, so adjust the number to suit your taste if you wish.

serves 4–6 | preparation 10 minutes | cooking 20 minutes

400–600 g/14 oz–1 lb 6 oz lamb mince
1 small onion, finely chopped (optional)
3 garlic cloves, crushed
4 cm/1½ in piece of root ginger, grated
1¼ tsp salt
1½ tsp cumin seeds
1½ tsp tandoori masala

1½ tsp garam masala
2 green finger chillies, finely chopped
a large handful of fresh coriander
  (cilantro), chopped
1 tbsp oil
1 lemon or lime, sliced, to garnish

1 Place all the ingredients except the coriander and oil in a bowl. Add half the coriander and mix together by hand, using the oil to moisten your hands.

2 Mould the mixture into long sausages around metal or soaked wooden skewers. Grill (broil) or barbecue for about 15–20 minutes, turning occasionally, until cooked.

3 Garnish with the remaining coriander and the lemon or lime slices and serve.

SERVING SUGGESTIONS AND TIPS

- Enjoy this dish with Pudina Dahi (see page 136) as a starter or wrap in fresh chapattis, tortilla wraps, naans or pittas and add yoghurt and salad for a more substantial meal.

Tandoori Murgi

TANDOORI CHICKEN

Popular in non-vegetarian Punjabi households and, in our house, often a Saturday night treat! This versatile dish of chicken pieces marinated in creamy yoghurt with delicate tandoori spices needs very little preparation. The potato wedges make a great accompaniment. Two chillies gives a medium dish.

serves 4–6 | preparation 10 minutes | marinating 30 minutes | cooking 30–40 minutes

150 ml/¼ pt/small pot of plain yoghurt
1 tsp salt
2 tbsp tandoori masala
1 tbsp tandoori paste
2 green finger chillies, finely chopped
3 bay leaves

8 skinless chicken drumsticks or pieces
4 medium unpeeled potatoes, cut into
  thick wedges
2 tbsp olive oil
a handful of chopped fresh coriander
  (cilantro), to garnish

1 Preheat the oven to 180°C/350°F/gas 4/fan oven 160°C.

2 Mix together the yoghurt, salt, spices, chillies and bay leaves. Mix in the chicken and potato wedges and chill for 30 minutes. Brush a baking (cookie) sheet lightly with the oil.

3 Using tongs, remove the chicken from the marinade and place on the baking sheet. Cook for about 30–40 minutes until cooked through, turning occasionally and basting with the remaining marinade.

4 Garnish with the coriander and serve.

SERVING SUGGESTIONS AND TIPS

- Enjoy this dish as a snack with Pudina Dahi (see page 136), lemon slices and a salad, or as part of a main course with rice, Tarwala Dahi (see page 136) and fresh roti.

- For a vegetarian version, substitute paneer for the chicken, or just add (bell) peppers and onion wedges.

- The chicken can also be barbecued on skewers or chargrilled.

Lassan Ki Murgi

GARLIC CHICKEN WINGS

This recipe uses tender chicken wings blended with aromatic spices and a fantastic extra garlic flavour. They are best eaten with your hands so that you can lick your fingers, but be warned – they are highly addictive! This dish is made using at least 4 chillies but the Greek yoghurt calms the chillies to give a medium-hot result.

serves 4–6 | preparation 10 minutes | marinating 1 hour | cooking 30 minutes

8–10 garlic cloves
6 cm/2½ in piece of root ginger
4 green finger chillies
3 tsp salt
2 tsp paprika
1 tsp freshly ground black pepper
2 tsp tandoori masala
2 tsp Madras curry paste from a jar

4 tbsp Greek or plain yoghurt
1 kg/2¼ lb skinless chicken wings, washed
5 tbsp olive oil
2 onions, sliced
2 tsp garam masala
a large handful of fresh coriander (cilantro), chopped

1 Whiz together the garlic, ginger, chillies, salt, paprika, pepper, tandoori masala, Madras curry paste and yoghurt in a grinder or blender to make a smooth paste. You may need to add 1–2 tbsp of water to get the right consistency.

2 Rub this paste into the chicken wings, cover and leave to marinate in the fridge for at least 1 hour or until ready to cook.

3 Heat the oil in a large saucepan or wok for 1 minute, then add the onions and cook for about 3 minutes until they are soft and translucent.

4 Add the chicken wings with the marinade and cook over a medium heat for 15 minutes, tossing constantly.

5 Add the garam masala and cook for a further 10 minutes until this spice has blended into the chicken wings.

6 Add the coriander, then transfer to a serving dish and serve.

SERVING SUGGESTIONS AND TIPS

• Enjoy this dish with hot naans and cooling yoghurt.

• Alternatively, cook under a preheated grill (broiler) for 20–25 minutes or in a preheated oven at 200°C/400°F/gas 6/fan oven 180°C for 35–40 minutes, turning occasionally. Omit the onions and add the garam masala to the marinade.

Khass Khaney Ki Cheej – Sabji

SOMETHING MAIN – VEGETABLES

The majority of people living in India have a vegetarian diet. Therefore, for vegetarians Punjabi food is a paradise of heavenly food full of flavour and vibrant colour, with countless main ingredient choices.

In our homes these exciting vegetable dishes – otherwise known as sabjis – are served simply with Indian breads, typically chapattis, or rice, our favourites being Bhindi Bhaji (Ladies' Fingers, see page 44), Bhartha Bengan (Mashed Aubergines, see page 56), Satpal's Sada Bahar Saag (Satpal's All-weather Mixed Greens, see page 59) and Thari Wale Kaju te Paneer (Cashew Nut and Paneer Curry, see page 52). For grand occasions, these vegetarian dishes are served with richer breads such as naans and bhaturey.

Mirchi Paneer te Rangi Shimla Mirch

CHILLI PANEER WITH COLOURFUL PEPPERS

Paneer is an Indian soft cheese, which tastes like a milky curd. This is a very colourful vegetarian starter dish, which has a great moist, spongy texture and gushes flavour. For a more authentic taste, try making your own paneer instead of using ready made (see page 16). Two chillies gives a medium-hot result.

serves 4–6 | preparation 10 minutes | marinating 20 minutes | cooking 15 minutes

400 g/14 oz bought or home-made
  paneer, chopped into 2 cm/³/₄ in cubes
1¹/₄ tsp salt
1 tsp paprika
1¹/₂ tsp garam masala
3¹/₂ tbsp olive oil
1 onion, thinly sliced

3 garlic cloves, crushed
5 cm/2 in piece of root ginger, grated
2 green finger chilles, chopped
2 (bell) peppers (any colour), seeded and
  thinly sliced
a handful of chopped fresh coriander
  (cilantro) and 1 lime, to garnish

1 Place the paneer cubes in a mixing bowl with the salt, paprika and garam masala. Add half the oil and mix to bind all the ingredients together.

2 Cover the bowl with clingfilm (plastic wrap) and leave to marinate in the fridge for at least 20 minutes or until ready to cook.

3 Heat the remaining oil in a frying pan (skillet) or wok for 1 minute, add the onion and stir-fry for about 3 minutes over a medium heat until it becomes soft and translucent.

4 Add the garlic, ginger and chillies and fry (sauté) lightly for 2 minutes.

5 Add the marinated paneer cubes and fry lightly for 5 minutes until they are lightly golden brown on all sides.

6 Mix the sliced peppers into the rest of ingredients and fry lightly for 4–5 minutes.

7 Garnish with the coriander, add a squeeze of lime juice and serve.

SERVING SUGGESTIONS AND TIPS

- Enjoy with hot naans and Mr T's Tazhee Pudina Chutney (see page 133).

- As a variation, substitute two 250 g/9 oz packs of tofu for the paneer.

Bhindi Bhaji

LADIES' FINGERS

Synonymous with Indian food, okra is an authentic, vibrantly green Indian vegetable. Simply prepared with flavoured onions, it creates a gorgeous dish. The okra must be dried after washing otherwise it becomes slimy when cooked. Use two chillies for a medium heat, or adjust the number according to your taste.

serves 4–6 | preparation 10 minutes | cooking 15 minutes

400 g/14 oz okra (ladies' fingers)
3 tbsp olive oil
1 tsp cumin seeds
1 large onion, chopped
2 garlic cloves, chopped
5 cm/2 in piece of root ginger, grated

2 green finger chillies, chopped
1 tsp salt
1 tsp garam masala
a handful of chopped fresh coriander
 (cilantro), to garnish

1 Wash and thoroughly dry each okra, then chop into 2.5 cm/1 in lengths.

2 Heat the oil in a frying pan (skillet) for 1 minute. Add the cumin seeds and leave for about 1–2 minutes until they start popping.

3 Add the onion, garlic, ginger and chillies and fry (sauté) gently over a medium heat for just 2 minutes.

4 Add the okra and stir and toss well for 5 minutes over a medium heat to coat with the rest of the ingredients.

5 Add the salt, reduce the heat to low and leave to cook for a further 4–5 minutes.

6 Stir in the garam masala and serve garnished with the coriander.

SERVING SUGGESTIONS AND TIPS

- Enjoy this dish with chapattis, crispy flat breads, a yoghurt dish such as Masala Dahi (see page 138) or Tarwala Dahi (see page 136), and Gajar Ka Achar (see page 137).

- As a variation, you could make Bhindi Bhaji te Nariyal Curry. Follow the recipe as above, but at step 4 toss well for 2 minutes, then add 1 cup of canned coconut milk and 1 tsp turmeric.

Tari Wale Aloo Chole

POTATO AND CHICK PEA CURRY

A very popular Punjabi vegetarian dish, this can be prepared straight from your cupboard ingredients. The result is delicious, nutty chick peas in a heavenly rich curry sauce with tomatoes. If you like a hotter, dish, you can use three chillies – or four if you like it very hot indeed!

serves 4–6 | preparation 10 minutes | cooking 25 minutes

1 tsp cumin seeds
4 tbsp olive oil
2 onions, chopped
3 garlic cloves, chopped
4 cm/1½ in piece of root ginger, chopped
1½ tsp salt
1 tsp turmeric
1½ tsp tandoori masala
1½ tsp chana masala (optional)
2 large tomatoes, chopped

2 green finger chillies, chopped
1 medium potato, peeled and chopped
　into 3 cm/1¼ in pieces
600 g/1 lb 6 oz/1½ large cans of chick
　peas (garbanzos), drained and washed
2 cups water
1 tsp garam masala
a handful of chopped fresh coriander
　(cilantro), to garnish

1　Dry-fry the cumin seeds in large, deep saucepan over a medium heat for 1 minute. Add the oil and cook for a further 1 minute.

2　Add the onions, garlic and ginger and cook for about 3 minutes until golden brown.

3　Stir in the salt, turmeric, tandoori masala and chana masala and cook for 2 minutes, stirring constantly.

4　Add the tomatoes and chillies and heat for about 5 minutes until the oil bubbles to the top and separates from the rest of the ingredients.

5　Stir in the potatoes, then the chick peas and heat through for 2 minutes.

6　Add the water, bring to boil, then simmer over a low heat for about 20 minutes.

7　Stir in the garam masala to thicken the sauce further. Remove from the heat and serve garnished with the coriander.

SERVING SUGGESTIONS AND TIPS

- Enjoy this dish with Masala Chawal (see page 98), Tarwala Dahi (see page 136), Tazhee Punjabi Roti (see page 104) or Ghee Wala Sada Paratha (see page 106).

- You could use a 230 g/8 oz/small can of chopped tomatoes instead of fresh.

SOMETHING MAIN – VEGETABLES

Paneer Bhurji

SCRAMBLED PANEER

This is a very simple, fresh and healthy Indian dish, suitable for just about any time of day. Use ready-made paneer if you are short of time, but you can make your own (see page 16) for a more authentic flavour. We suggest using just one chilli, but you can always use more if you prefer a hotter dish.

serves 4–6 | preparation 10 minutes | cooking 20 minutes

3 tbsp olive oil
1 red (bell) pepper, sliced
1 green pepper, sliced
a handful of frozen sweetcorn (corn)
a handful of fresh peas
1 tsp cumin seeds
1 onion, chopped
1 garlic clove, crushed

4 cm/1½ in piece of root ginger, grated
1 green finger chilli, chopped
1½ tsp salt
400 g/14 oz bought or home-made paneer, scrambled with a fork
a handful of chopped fresh coriander (cilantro), to garnish

1   Heat 1 tbsp of the oil in a frying pan (skillet) or wok for 1 minute, add the peppers and gently stir-fry over a medium heat for about 3 minutes. Remove from the pan and set aside.

2   Half-cook the sweetcorn and peas, then drain and set aside.

3   Using the same saucepan, heat the remaining oil. Add the cumin seeds and onion and cook for about 3 minutes over a medium heat until the onion is soft and translucent.

4   Add the garlic, ginger, chilli and salt and fry (sauté) lightly for about 2 minutes until golden brown.

5   Add the paneer and cook lightly for 5 minutes, turning the paneer so it mixes in with all the other ingredients. It should start to become a golden-brown colour.

6   Mix in the peppers, sweetcorn and peas. Cook lightly for 5 minutes.

7   Garnish with the coriander before serving.

SERVING SUGGESTIONS AND TIPS

- This is a versatile lunch dish stuffed in a naan or wrapped in a tortilla with salad and Mr T's Tazhee Pudina Chutney (see page 133). Or try it as a main course accompanied with a second curry, rice, chapattis and a yoghurt dish.

Soya Keema te Matter

MINCED SOYA AND PEAS

Soya products are an enticing alternative to meat in Indian dishes. It's just as quick and easy to cook as minced meats and highly nutritious. Why not try this on your friends and see if they notice the difference? We recommend two chillies for a medium result, but you can spice it up with more if you prefer.

serves 4–6 | preparation 10 minutes | cooking 40 minutes

4 tbsp olive oil
1½ tsp cumin seeds
1 large onion, chopped
3 garlic cloves, crushed
5 cm/2 in piece of root ginger, chopped
2 green finger chillies, chopped
5 tbsp water
4 tomatoes, chopped
1½ tsp salt

1 tsp turmeric
1¼ tsp paprika
1¼ tsp curry powder
1½ tsp garam masala
450 g/1 lb fresh or frozen soya mince
½ cup frozen peas
1 cup water
a handful of chopped fresh coriander
(cilantro), to garnish

1 Heat the oil in a large saucepan for 1 minute. Add the cumin seeds and listen for them to start popping (this should take about 1–2 minutes).

2 Add the onion and cook for about 3 minutes over a medium heat until soft.

3 Add the garlic, ginger and chillies and fry (sauté) gently for about 1 minute. Add 4–5 tbsp of water and cook for a further 4 minutes until the ingredients become softer and paste-like.

4 Add the tomatoes and cook for about 5 minutes until the oil bubbles to the top.

5 Add the salt, turmeric, paprika, curry powder and garam masala and cook for 2 minutes until the spices have blended together. Add the soya mince and peas and stir for 2 minutes until all the ingredients are blended and heated through.

6 Add the water and bring to the boil. Cover and simmer over a low heat for about 20 minutes.

7 Garnish with the coriander and serve.

SERVING SUGGESTIONS AND TIPS

- Enjoy this dish with Sabji Biryani (see page 96) or Tazhee Punjabi Roti (see page 104), Tarwala Dahi (see page 136) and Sona's Desi Salad (see page 29).

Masala Baby Bengan te Motae Aloo

SPICY BABY AUBERGINES AND THICK-CUT CHIPS

This is a traditional vegetarian dish with a Western influence, as you can tell from the accompanying thick-cut potato chips, which help to calm the exploding flavour of the tender baby aubergines. Why not try making your own masala mixes using the recipes on page 15?

serves 4–6 | preparation 10 minutes | cooking 30 minutes

1 large potato
8–10 small whole baby aubergines
   (eggplants)
6 tbsp olive oil
1¼ tsp salt
1 tsp turmeric
1½ tsp garam masala

1 tsp tandoori masala
1 tsp paprika
1 tsp hot chilli powder
1 tsp cumin seeds
a handful of chopped fresh coriander
   (cilantro), to garnish

1 Peel, wash and dry the potato and cut into 2 cm/¾ in thick chips about 5 cms/ 2 in long. Wash and then thoroughly dry the aubergines. Using a sharp knife, make a slit down the middle of each, leaving 1–2 cm/1/2–¾ in at each end.

2 Heat 4 tbsp of the oil in a frying pan (skillet). Add the potato chips (fries) and shallow-fry for about 8 minutes, turning them over half-way through.

3 Meanwhile, in a mixing bowl, combine the salt, turmeric, garam masala, tandoori masala, paprika and chilli powder. Add half the remaining olive oil and mix well to make a paste.

4 Using your fingers, rub a teaspoonful of the paste on to the cut surfaces of each aubergine until they are completely covered inside. Leave to rest, covered with clingfilm (plastic wrap) until the chips are just over half-cooked.

5 Remove the chips from the frying pan and place in a bowl lined with kitchen paper (paper towels).

6 Wipe the frying pan with kitchen paper, then use it to dry-fry the cumin seeds for 1 minute over a medium heat. Add the remaining oil and heat through for 1 minute.

7 Add the baby aubergines, cover the frying pan and leave to cook over a medium heat for about 10 minutes, turning occasionally.

Photograph opposite:
Paprika Corn on the Cob (page 33)
with Cucumber Raita (page 136).

8 Turn the heat down to low and add the chips to the frying pan. Toss gently and cook for 8–10 minutes. Remove from heat and serve garnished with the coriander.

SERVING SUGGESTIONS AND TIPS

• Enjoy with chapattis, Masala Dahi (see page 138) and Nimbu Ka Achar (see page 140).

Sukhe Aloo

DRY POTATOES

A great comfort food, Sukhe Aloo manages to achieve what might be thought the impossible combination of dryness and moistness. You might have had this in Indian restaurants, where it is popularly called 'Bombay aloo', but making your own is so satisfying and any bought version will pale into insignificance.

serves 4 | preparation 5 minutes | cooking 25 minutes

4 medium potatoes, peeled and halved
4 tbsp olive oil
1 tsp cumin seeds
1 tsp mustard seeds
1 onion, thinly sliced

5 cm/2 in piece of root ginger, grated
1¼ tsp salt
a handful of chopped fresh coriander (cilantro) and crushed dried red chillies (optional), to garnish

1 Parboil the potatoes in salted boiling water for about 5 minutes. Drain, allow to cool, then chop into roughly 2.5 cm/1 in cubes.

2 Heat the oil in a saucepan for 1 minute. Add the cumin and mustard seeds and wait until they start popping (this should take about 1–2 minutes).

3 Add the onion, ginger and salt and fry (sauté) over a medium heat for 3 minutes until the onions are turning golden brown.

4 Add the potatoes and stir well to coat with the rest of the ingredients. Reduce the heat and continue cooking for 12–15 minutes, stirring occasionally.

5 Garnish with the coriander and, for extra bite, sprinkle with dried red chillies.

SERVING SUGGESTIONS AND TIPS

• Enjoy with simple chapattis or rice, or serve as part of a vegetarian selection.

Photograph opposite:
Three-colour Vegetables (page 51) with Tomato and Onion Yoghurt (page 138).

Tari Wale Khumban te Shaley

MUSHROOM AND SWEETCORN CURRY

For this delicious dish, whole button mushrooms and sweetcorn are covered in a rich, spicy, tomato masala sauce. It's surprisingly quick and easy to make, yet tempting and filling. We suggest using two chillies for a medium-hot dish but if you like your food spicier, you can add one more.

serves 4–6 | preparation 10 minutes | cooking 30 minutes

3 tbsp olive oil
1 tsp cumin seeds
1 tsp mustard seeds
2 onions, chopped
2–3 garlic cloves, crushed
5 cm/2 in piece of root ginger, chopped
2 green finger chillies, chopped
4 tomatoes, chopped
1½ tsp salt

1 tsp turmeric
1 tsp paprika
1 tsp curry powder
1½ tsp garam masala
400 g/14 oz whole button mushrooms
250 g/9 oz/medium can of sweetcorn (corn)
1½ cups water
a handful of fresh coriander (cilantro), chopped

1 Heat the oil in a large saucepan for 2 minutes. Add the cumin seeds and mustard seeds and listen for them to start popping (this should take about 1–2 minutes).

2 Add the onions and cook over a medium heat for about 3 minutes until they are soft and translucent.

3 Add the garlic, ginger and chillies and fry (sauté) gently for about 2 minutes.

4 Add 4–5 tbsp of water and cook for a further 4 minutes until the ingredients become softer and paste-like.

5 Add the tomatoes and heat for about 5 minutes until the oil bubbles to the top and separates from the rest of the ingredients.

6 Add the salt, turmeric, paprika, curry powder and garam masala and cook for 2 minutes until the spices have blended together.

7 Add the whole button mushrooms and sweetcorn. Stir and heat through for 2 minutes.

8 Add the water and bring to the boil. Cover, then simmer over a low heat for about 8–10 minutes.

9 Add the coriander just before serving.

- Enjoy this with your favourite rice dish or chapattis, naans, Masala Dahi (see page 138) and Sona's Desi Salad (see page 29).

Teen Rangi Sabji

THREE-COLOUR VEGETABLES

A vibrant dish of red, yellow and green vegetables bursting with flavour, this recipe uses no onion, allowing all the flavours of the masala and spices to come through. It's so quick and easy to make and you can always try using different vegetables in other colours. Use one chilli for a mild dish, two for medium.

serves 4 | preparation 10 minutes | cooking 10 minutes

1 tsp cumin seeds
4 tbsp olive oil
³/₄ tsp turmeric
³/₄ tsp salt
1–2 green finger chillies, chopped
³/₄ tsp Madras curry paste
1 large red or orange (bell) pepper, cut
   into thin strips

200 g/7 oz packet of baby sweetcorn
   (corn)
3 tbsp water
200 g/7 oz packet of mangetout
   (snow peas)
1¼ tbsp garam masala
a large handful of chopped fresh
   coriander (cilantro) leaves or 2 tbsp
   dried fenugreek leaves

1 In a frying pan (skillet), dry roast the cumin seeds for 1 minute over a medium heat. Add the oil, increase the heat slightly and add the turmeric, salt, chillies and Madras curry paste. Stir for 1 minute.

2 Add the sliced pepper and sweetcorn and stir-fry for 3 minutes.

3 Add the water and mangetout and cook for a further 5–7 minutes, stirring frequently.

4 Remove the frying pan from the heat and add the garam masala and coriander or fenugreek leaves. Mix well and serve.

SERVING SUGGESTIONS AND TIPS

- Serve with rice or chapattis and Masala Dahi (see page 138).

- As a variation, add 1 tbsp of creamed coconut and 1–1¹/₂ tbsp each of plain yoghurt and single (light) cream just before adding the garam masala.

Thari Wale Kaju te Paneer

CASHEW NUT AND PANEER CURRY

This is a classic vegetarian dish with a slight twist. Traditionally, it's made with peas, but here we use cashew nuts instead to create a richer and more regal dish. The result is irresistible – fried milky paneer bites combined with cashews, all bathed in a magnificent, spicy, mouth-watering masala sauce.

serves 4–6 | preparation 10 minutes | cooking 50 minutes

1½ tsp cumin seeds
4 tbsp olive oil
2 onions, chopped
3–4 garlic cloves, crushed or ¾ tsp garlic paste
4 cm/1½ in piece of root ginger, crushed, or ¾ tsp ginger paste
2–4 green finger chillies, chopped
1½ tsp salt
1½ tsp turmeric

1 tsp Madras curry paste (optional)
1½ tsp tandoori masala
4 tomatoes, chopped
250 g/9 oz fried paneer cubes (see page 16)
½ cup unsalted raw cashew nuts
2 cups water
1½ tsp garam masala
a handful of fresh coriander (cilantro), chopped

1 Dry-roast the cumin seeds in a saucepan for 1 minute until they begin to pop.

2 Add the oil, then the onions and cook for about 4 minutes over a medium heat until they are soft and translucent.

3 Add the garlic, ginger and chillies and fry (sauté) lightly for 2 minutes.

4 Add the salt, turmeric, Madras curry paste, if using, and tandoori masala and cook for 1 minute until the spices have cooked and are blended together.

5 Add the tomatoes and cook for about 5 minutes, stirring frequently, until they blend to form a smooth paste. Continue until the oil separates from the paste and rises to the top.

6 Add the paneer cubes and cashew nuts and stir for about 2 minutes until all the ingredients are blended.

7 Add the water and bring to the boil. Cover, then simmer over a low heat for 35 minutes until the sauce is rich and thick.

8 Stir in the garam masala and coriander and serve.

- Enjoy this dish with chapattis, naans, tortilla wraps or rice and a yoghurt accompaniment.

- As a variation, fried soya mince pieces can be substituted for the paneer and traditional peas can be substituted for the cashew nuts.

- For a drier curry, add only ³/₄ cup of water.

- If you don't want to make your own fried paneer cubes, cut cubes from a bought block and fry until golden. Or use pre-packed tofu instead.

Kadoo Kas Patha Gobi, Gajar te Matter

GRATED CABBAGE, CARROT AND PEAS

Ginger is an essential ingredient in all Indian cabbage and cauliflower recipes as it enables these vegetables to be easily digested. This is one of Babita's mum's inventions to feed us our veggie quota. Getting your healthy five-portions-a-day is so easy with Indian vegetarian dishes!

serves 4–6 | preparation 10 minutes | cooking 20 minutes

4 tbsp olive oil
1 tsp cumin seeds
1 tsp mustard seeds
1 onion, thinly sliced
10 cm/4 in piece of root ginger, grated
1¼ tsp salt

1 large cabbage, grated
2 large carrots, chopped
2 handfuls of fresh or frozen peas
a handful of chopped fresh coriander
    (cilantro), to garnish

1 Heat the oil in a saucepan for 1 minute. Add the cumin and mustard seeds and wait until they start popping (this will take about 1–2 minutes).

2 Add the onion, ginger and salt and fry (sauté) gently over a medium heat for 2 minutes until the onion turns golden brown.

3 Add the cabbage, carrots and peas and stir well to coat with the rest of the ingredients. Cook over a low heat for about 12–15 minutes, tossing occasionally.

4 Garnish with the coriander and serve.

SERVING SUGGESTIONS AND TIPS

- Enjoy this dish with chapattis, a yoghurt dish and Gajar Ka Achar (see page 137).

Aloo Palak Ki Sabji

POTATO AND SPINACH VEGETABLES

*A traditional Punjabi recipe combining delicious and mouth-wateringly tender baby
spinach leaves with temptingly sweet potatoes, which are sweated in garlic, ginger
and masala spices. A great one for vegetarians, it makes a dish that is so delicious
yet quick and easy to conjure up.*

serves 4 | preparation 10 minutes | cooking 20 minutes

6–8 salad potatoes or 2 medium potatoes
1 tbsp cumin seeds
4 tbsp olive oil
1 large onion, finely chopped
4 cm/1½ in piece of root ginger, grated,
  or ¾ tsp ginger paste
4 garlic cloves, crushed, or ¾ tsp garlic
  paste

1¼ tsp turmeric
1¼ tsp salt
2–3 green finger chillies, chopped
300 g/11 oz/large bag of baby spinach
  leaves, roughly chopped
1½ tsp garam masala
a large handful of fresh coriander
  (cilantro), chopped

1 Peel the potatoes and cut into 4 cm/1½ in cubes.

2 Dry-roast the cumin seeds in a saucepan for 1 minute. Add the oil and onion and
  fry (sauté) until golden brown Add the ginger and garlic and cook for a further
  3 minutes.

3 Stir in the turmeric, salt and chillies. Add the potatoes and cook for 2 minutes,
  stirring occasionally.

4 Add the spinach and mix well. Cover and cook for 15 minutes over a medium heat
  until most of the water from the spinach has been absorbed and the potatoes are
  cooked through. If any water remains at the end, remove the lid and cook for a
  further 2 minutes.

5 Remove from the heat, add the garam masala and coriander, mix and serve.

SERVING SUGGESTIONS AND TIPS

- Serve with hot chapattis and Masala Dahi (see page 138).
- As a variation, substitute baby aubergines (eggplants) for the spinach and add
  2 large tomatoes, chopped, to make Bengan te Aloo – delicious!

Sab Ki Pasand Aloo Gobi Sabji

EVERYONE'S FAVOURITE POTATO AND CAULIFLOWER VEGETABLES

Another Punjabi classic, this dish is cooked in most, if not all, Indian households. Crisp cauliflower florets are complemented with appetising soft, golden potatoes, all spiced up and best served fresh and hot. This is another wonderfully satisfying dish that vegetarians won't be able to keep to themselves!

serves 4–6 | preparation 10 minutes | cooking 15 minutes

4 tbsp olive oil

2 medium onions, chopped

3–4 garlic cloves, crushed, or ³/₄ tsp garlic paste

4 cm/1¹/₂ in piece of ginger, grated, or ³/₄ tsp ginger paste

1¹/₄ tsp salt

1¹/₄ tsp turmeric

2–3 green finger chillies, chopped

3 medium potatoes, peeled and chopped into 2.5 cm/1 in cubes

1 medium cauliflower, cut into florets

2 tsp garam masala

a large handful of fresh coriander, chopped

1 tbsp dried fenugreek leaves (optional)

1 Heat the oil in a large saucepan over a medium heat. Add the onions and fry (sauté) for 1 minute. Add the garlic and ginger and fry until golden brown.

2 Add the salt, turmeric and chillies and cook for 1 minute.

3 Add the potatoes, cauliflower and garam masala. Mix well and cook over a low heat, stirring occasionally to ensure even cooking, for about 12–15 minutes until the potatoes soften.

4 Remove the pan from the heat. Add the coriander and fenugreek leaves, if using, mix together and serve.

SERVING SUGGESTIONS AND TIPS

- Serve with fresh chapattis, yoghurt, rice and salad as accompaniments.

Bengan Bhartha

MASHED AUBERGINES

A traditional Punjabi dish made with fresh aubergines and fresh tomatoes, this recipe has been adapted by Anju Aunty by burning off the aubergine skin, giving it a very distinctive smoked flavour. Instead of using bought masala mixes, why not try making your own using our recipes on page 15?

serves 4 | preparation 15 minutes | cooking 20 minutes

1 large aubergine (eggplant)
1¹/₂ tsp cumin seeds
3 tbsp olive oil
1 large onion, chopped
2 garlic cloves, chopped
4 cm/1¹/₂ in piece of root ginger, grated
1¹/₄ tsp salt

1¹/₂ tsp turmeric
1¹/₂ tsp garam masala
1 tsp tandoori masala
1 tomato, chopped
2 green finger chillies, chopped
a handful of chopped fresh coriander
   (cilantro), to garnish

1 Prick the aubergine several times with a fork and place it under a hot grill (broiler) on full heat for about 15 minutes, turning three or four times, until the skin is cooked and crispy all over. Remove from the grill and leave to cool.

2 Slice the aubergine in half and scoop out the soft inside into a bowl. Discard the skin and mash the flesh with a fork.

3 In a saucepan, dry-fry the cumin seeds for 1 minute, then add the oil and heat through for 1 minute. Add the onion, garlic and ginger and stir constantly until golden brown.

4 Add the salt, turmeric, garam masala and tandoori masala. Cook, stirring, for 2 minutes over a low heat. Add the tomato and chillies and stir for a further 5 minutes.

5 Add the mashed aubergine, mix and heat through over a low heat for 10 minutes.

6 Remove from heat, garnish with the coriander and serve.

SERVING SUGGESTIONS AND TIPS

- Enjoy with fresh hot chapattis, Khooshboo Elachi Chawal (see page 98) and Masala Dahi (see page 138).

- To make classic Aloo Bengan, omit steps 1 and 2 and cut the aubergine into bite-sized pieces, leaving the skin on. Add to the pan at step 4 with 1 chopped potato.

Punjabi Sabji Wale Kofte

PUNJABI VEGETABLE BALLS

*Grated potato and chick pea flour balls are here spiced up Punjabi style with garlic,
ginger and tandoori spices, then fried. These are really easy to make and are
delicious served as a snack or as part of a main meal in hot tortilla wraps or naans.
Remember, you can add more or fewer chillies to suit your taste.*

serves 4–6 | preparation 10 minutes | cooking 20 minutes

For the kofte
2 large baking potatoes, grated
6 tbsp rice flour
4 tbsp chick pea (garbanzo) flour
2 tsp cumin seeds
1¹/₂ tsp salt
2 tsp garam masala
2 green finger chillies, finely chopped
2¹/₂ cups vegetable oil for deep-frying,
  plus extra for greasing

For the sauce
1¹/₂ tsp cumin seeds
4 tbsp vegetable oil
2 onions, finely chopped (optional)

3–4 garlic cloves, crushed, or ³/₄ tsp
  garlic paste
4 cm/1¹/₂ in piece of root ginger, grated,
  or ³/₄ tsp ginger paste
2–3 green finger chillies, finely chopped
1¹/₄ tsp turmeric
1 tsp salt
1¹/₄ tsp tandoori masala
3 large tomatoes, chopped
1¹/₂ tsp garam masala
1 cup water
a large handful of chopped fresh
  coriander (cilantro), to garnish

1 Blend all the kofte ingredients and shape into balls with lightly oiled hands.

2 Heat the oil and deep-fry the kofte for about 6–8 minutes until crispy and golden
  brown. Remove and drain on kitchen paper (paper towels). Set aside.

3 To make the sauce, dry-roast the cumin seeds in a saucepan for 1 minute. Add
  the oil, onions, garlic, ginger and chillies and fry (sauté) until softened.

4 Add the turmeric, salt, tandoori masala and tomatoes and simmer until the oil
  rises to the top.

5 Add the garam masala and water. Bring to the boil and simmer for about 15
  minutes until the sauce thickens. Add the kofte and heat through. Serve
  garnished with the coriander.

SERVING SUGGESTIONS AND TIPS

- Enjoy this dish with naans, chapattis, tortilla wraps, pittas or rice.

Mummyji's Thari Wale Aande

MUM'S EXTRAORDINARY EGG CURRY

This dish is a great comfort food that Babita's mum used to cook for her when she was a child. Before serving the egg curry, cut a few of the whole eggs into halves and make sure they are coated very thoroughly in the curry masala sauce. You'll find that they just melt in your mouth!

serves 4–6 | preparation 10 minutes | cooking 30 minutes

8 eggs
4 tbsp olive oil
2 onions, chopped
4 cm/1½ in piece of root ginger, grated
1½ tsp salt
1 tsp freshly ground black pepper
½ tsp turmeric
1½ tsp Madras curry powder (optional)

1 tsp paprika
3 tomatoes, chopped
2 medium potatoes, peeled and cut into
  2.5 cm/1 in cubes
2 cups water
1½ tsp garam masala
a handful of fresh coriander (cilantro),
  chopped

1 Boil the eggs for 8 minutes, then drain and place in a bowl of cold water. When cool enough to handle, remove the shells and leave the eggs to cool.

2 Heat the oil in a large saucepan for 1 minute. Add the onions and cook for about 3 minutes over a medium heat until they are soft and translucent.

3 Add the ginger and fry (sauté) lightly for 1 minute.

4 Add the salt, pepper, turmeric, Madras curry powder, if using, and paprika and cook for 1 minute until spices have cooked and blended together.

5 Add the tomatoes and heat for about 5 minutes until the oil rises to the top and separates from the rest of the ingredients.

6 Add the hard-boiled (hard-cooked) eggs and potato cubes and stir for 2 minutes until all ingredients are blended and heated through.

7 Add the water and bring to the boil.

8 Add the garam masala, then cover and simmer over a low heat for 15 minutes.

9 Add the coriander and serve.

SERVING SUGGESTIONS AND TIPS

• Enjoy this dish with rice, peas and yoghurt.

Satpal's Sada Bahar Saag

SATPAL'S ALL-WEATHER MIXED GREENS

A Northern Indian favourite, traditionally saag is mustard leaves (saron da saag) boiled down until the water evaporates to give a silky texture. A mixture of fried onions with ginger and garlic and – naturally! – chillies complete the dish. Our recipe here is Win's mum's version, which uses greens available all year round.

serves 6–8 | preparation 10 minutes | cooking 1¼ hours

2 x 300 g/11 oz/large bags of baby
   spinach leaves
1 medium-sized broccoli stem
2 large handfuls of fresh coriander
   (cilantro)
a large handful of fresh fenugreek leaves
1½ tsp salt
2 tbsp butter or ghee
3 green finger chillies, finely chopped

1½ cups yellow cornmeal
For the tharka
4 tbsp butter
1 large onion, finely chopped
6 garlic cloves, crushed, or 1½ tsp
   garlic paste
7.5 cm/3 in piece of root ginger, grated,
   or 1½ tsp ginger paste

1 Wash the spinach, broccoli, coriander and fenugreek thoroughly in a colander. Drain and chop finely.

2 Place in a large heavy-based saucepan with 4 cups of water, the salt, butter or ghee and the chillies. Bring to the boil, cover and simmer over a low heat for about 1 hour, stirring occasionally.

3 When all the water has been absorbed, remove the pan from the heat and mash the greens with a potato masher.

4 Mix the cornmeal with 1 cup of water and add to the boiled greens. Again using the potato masher, mash and mix together. Return the pan to the heat, add a further 1 cup of water and cook for 5 minutes.

5 To make the tharka, heat the butter in a frying pan (skillet). Add the onion, garlic and ginger and cook until golden brown. Add to the saag, mix well and serve.

SERVING SUGGESTIONS AND TIPS

- Serve with Sadi Maki Ki Roti (see page 110) or chapattis, and plain yoghurt or Masala Dahi (see page 138).

Soya Kofte

SOYA MEATBALLS

A tasty and healthy alternative to lamb meatball curry, this delicious dish is made in a traditional delicious Punjabi sauce. It will be enjoyed not just by vegetarians but by anyone who enjoys a tasty curry. Use one chilli for a mild curry, two for medium, three for hot and four for extra hot.

serves 4–6 | preparation 5 minutes | cooking 40 minutes

4 tbsp olive oil
1½ tsp cumin seeds
2 onions, chopped
3 garlic cloves, crushed, or ½ tsp garlic paste
4 cm/1½ in piece of root ginger, grated, or ¾ tsp ginger paste
1–4 green finger chillies, chopped
4 tomatoes, skinned and chopped

1½ tsp salt
1 tsp turmeric
1½ tsp paprika
1½ tsp curry powder
1½ tsp garam masala
450 g/1 lb soya meatballs, fresh or frozen
1½ cups of boiling water
a handful of fresh coriander (cilantro), chopped

1 Heat the oil in a large saucepan for 2 minutes. Add the cumin seeds and fry (sauté) for 1–2 minutes until they start popping.

2 Add the onions and cook for about 3 minutes over a medium heat until they are soft and translucent.

3 Add the garlic, ginger and chillies and fry gently over a medium heat for about 2 minutes.

4 Add 4–5 tbsp of cold water and mix to a soft paste. Cook for a further 4 minutes.

5 Add the tomatoes and heat for about 5 minutes until the oil rises to the top and separates from the rest of the ingredients.

6 Add the salt, turmeric, paprika, curry powder and garam masala and cook for 2 minutes until the spices are cooked and blended together.

7 Add the soya meatballs and heat through for 2 minutes, stirring gently, until they are bathed in the sauce.

8 Add the boiling water and bring to the boil. Cover and simmer over a low heat for about 20 minutes.

9 Add the coriander just before serving.

- Enjoy this dish with any rice, Tarwala Dahi (see page 136) and fresh chapattis, naans or tortilla wraps.

Shahi Gobi

MAJESTIC CAULIFLOWER

Taught to us by Win's mum, a delightful variation on the better-known aloo gobi. This dish merges crunchy grated cauliflower with luscious fresh coconut and wholesome crunchy cashew nuts to create something different – a heavenly and majestically spicy dish. We recommend 2–3 chillies, but you can always use fewer.

serves 4 | preparation 10 minutes | cooking 20 minutes

1 tbsp cumin seeds
1 tsp black mustard seeds (optional)
4 tbsp olive oil
2 onions, finely chopped
4 garlic cloves, crushed, or 3/4 tsp garlic paste
4 cm/1 1/2 in root ginger, grated, or 3/4 tsp ginger paste
1 1/2 tsp turmeric
1 1/4 tsp salt

2–3 green finger chillies, finely chopped
1 medium cauliflower, coarsely grated, or chopped in a blender
1/2 cup unsalted raw cashew nuts
2–3 tbsp unsweetened dessicated (shredded) or freshly grated coconut
1 1/2 tsp garam masala
a large handful of chopped fresh coriander (cilantro), to garnish

1 Dry-fry the cumin and mustard seeds in a large saucepan for 1 minute.

2 Add the oil, onion, garlic and ginger. Cook for about 3–4 minutes, stirring occasionally, until golden brown.

3 Add the turmeric, salt and chillies and cook for 1 minute, stirring constantly.

4 Add the cauliflower and cashew nuts and cook for 5 minutes, stirring occasionally.

5 Lower the heat, stir in the coconut and garam masala and cook for further 12–15 minutes, stirring occasionally, until the cauliflower is cooked through.

6 Remove from the heat, garnish with the coriander and serve.

SERVING SUGGESTIONS AND TIPS

- Serve with rice, chappatis and Tarwala Dahi (see page 136) as an accompaniment.

61

SOMETHING MAIN – VEGETABLES

Gajar, Aloo te Matter Ki Sabji

CARROTS, POTATOES AND PEAS

In this recipe, fresh seasonal vegetables are cooked in one pan to create a dry curry captured in wonderfully aromatic masala spices and topped off with fresh coriander – delicious and nutritious and a great way to eat your vegetables, especially carrots. Adjust the quantity of chilli to your own taste, if you wish.

serves 4–6 | **preparation 10 minutes** | **cooking 20 minutes**

4 tbsp olive oil

2 onions, chopped

3–4 garlic cloves, crushed, or ³/₄ tsp garlic paste

4 cm/1¹/₂ in piece of root ginger, grated, or ³/₄ tsp ginger paste

1¹/₄ tsp salt

1¹/₄ tsp turmeric

2–3 green finger chillies, chopped

6 carrots, diced or grated

2–3 medium potatoes, peeled and chopped

1¹/₄ tsp garam masala

1 cup peas, thawed if frozen

a good handful of fresh coriander (cilantro), chopped

1 tbsp dried fenugreek leaves (optional)

1 Heat the oil in a large saucepan over a medium heat. Add the onions and fry (sauté) for 1 minute.

2 Add the garlic and ginger and fry for 3–4 minutes until lightly browned.

3 Add the salt, turmeric and chillies and cook for 1 minute.

4 Add the carrots, potatoes and garam masala. Mix well and cook over a low heat for 10–15 minutes.

5 Add the peas and cook, stirring occasionally, until the potatoes are soft.

6 Remove from the heat and add the coriander and fenugreek leaves, if using. Mix together and serve.

SERVING SUGGESTIONS AND TIPS

- Serve with fresh chapattis, yoghurt, rice and salad as accompaniments.
- To make a change, you can substitute turnips for the carrots.

Desi Masala Noodles

INDIAN SPICY NOODLES

This is traditional spaghetti livened up with brightly coloured peppers, sweetcorn, mushrooms and exciting Indian spices to create an easy mouth-wateringly delicious and hearty dish. You could also add some plain or fried paneer cubes with the mushrooms and peppers.

serves 4–6 | preparation 5 minutes | cooking 20 minutes

4 tbsp olive oil
400 g/14 oz spaghetti
1 onion, chopped
2 garlic cloves, chopped
4 cm/1¹/₂ in piece of root ginger, grated
2 green finger chillies, chopped
1 red (bell) pepper, chopped
1 green pepper, chopped

8–10 small mushrooms, sliced
1¹/₂ tsp salt
a handful of frozen sweetcorn
1 tsp cumin seeds
1 tsp mustard seeds
a handful of chopped fresh coriander
  (cilantro), to garnish

1 Bring a saucepan of water to the boil and add 1 tbsp of the oil. Break the spaghetti in half, add to the pan and cook for half the time stated on the packet. Drain and set aside.

2 Heat 2 tbsp of the remaining olive oil in a large frying pan (skillet) or wok, add the onion and cook for about 3 minutes over a medium heat until soft and translucent.

3 Add the garlic, ginger and chillies and fry (sauté) lightly for 2 minutes until they are beginning to brown.

4 Add the peppers, mushrooms and salt and fry lightly for 5 minutes, stirring thoroughly to mix all the ingredients.

5 Add the half-cooked spaghetti and the sweetcorn and cook for a further 5 minutes, stirring frequently.

6 Pour the remaining olive oil into a separate frying pan and heat for 1 minute. Add the cumin and mustard seeds and fry for 2 minutes. Tip the seeds into the spaghetti mixture.

7 Garnish with the coriander and serve.

SERVING SUGGESTIONS AND TIPS

- Enjoy with Sukha Naryial Hare Mirch Chutney (see page 134).

Khass Khaney Ki Cheej – Machchi

SOMETHING MAIN – FISH

Most fish dishes originate from the south coast of India, where fish is found in abundance. Our inspiration for some of the fish recipes in this book has come from cooking with friends in Goa, where they use freshly caught fish and local spices to create sensational dishes.

Our wide range of fish dishes uses different blends of spices to create exquisite flavours that race across the palate. Our favourites include Meri Dost Ki Goan Machchi (My Friend's Goan Fish Curry, see page 66), which is quick to make and can be served any time, and, for an extravagant occasion, our Sabti Salmon Masala Machchi (Whole Salmon Masala Fish, see page 65) goes down a treat.

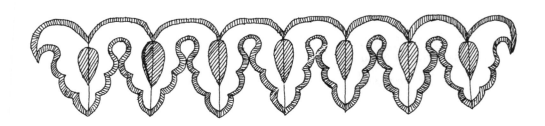

Sabti Salmon Masala Machchi

WHOLE SALMON MASALA FISH

A real stunner of a dish, safti salmon has a crispy, spicy coating on the outside and tender spiced salmon on the inside. It's quite an unusual dish and both looks and tastes impressive, although in fact it is easy to make. It makes a great centrepiece for dinner parties and special occasions.

serves 6 | **preparation 10 minutes** | **cooking 20 minutes**

1 large whole salmon (about 1 kg/2¼ lb), gutted but head and tail left on
½ tsp salt
½ tsp freshly ground black pepper
1 tsp turmeric
1½ tsp garam masala
1½ tsp paprika
½ tsp hot chilli powder

4 garlic cloves, thinly sliced
10 cm/4 in piece of root ginger, thinly sliced
1 lemon, thinly sliced
3 tbsp olive oil
a large handful of chopped fresh flatleaf parsley, to garnish

1 Wash the fish under cold running water. Working backwards from tail to head, rub the skin with a sharp knife to remove the scales.

2 Cut four or five slits about 5 cm/2 in deep into both sides of the fish.

3 Mix together the salt, pepper, turmeric, garam masala, paprika and chilli powder in a small bowl. Using your hands, rub this mixture into the fish, especially the slits.

4 Stuff a small handful of the garlic and ginger and the lemon slices into the slits of the fish and drizzle the fish on both sides with the olive oil.

5 Cook the salmon on a hot barbecue or under a preheated grill (broiler) for only 8–10 minutes on each side.

6 Garnish with the parsley and serve.

SERVING SUGGESTIONS

- Enjoy with rice, chapattis and salad as an accompaniment.

Meri Dost Ki Goan Machchi

MY FRIEND'S GOAN FISH CURRY

This traditional Goan dish is cooked by our friend Maria in a small village in South Goa using all local ingredients – fresh pomfret fish, coconut milk and plenty of spices. This gives a fantastic fusion of hot and spicy with a cool coconut-tasting fish curry. Monkfish and haddock are ideal as they are not prone to crumbling.

serves 4–6 | preparation 10 minutes | cooking 25 minutes

4 tbsp olive or coconut oil
1½ tsp cumin seeds
2 onions, finely chopped
3–4 garlic cloves, crushed
4 cm/1½ in piece of root ginger, finely chopped
2 green finger chillies, chopped
½ tsp salt
1 tsp turmeric
1½ tsp garam masala

½ tsp freshly ground black pepper
2 tomatoes, chopped
½ cup coconut milk (from a can or dried)
2 tbsp Greek yoghurt
6 fresh or frozen skinless fish fillets (about 400–600 g/14 oz–1 lb 6 oz)
juice of 1 lemon
juice of 1 lime
a handful of chopped fresh coriander (cilantro), to garnish

1 Heat the oil in a large saucepan over a medium heat for 1 minute. Add the cumin seeds and onions and cook for about 3 minutes until the onions are soft and translucent.

2 Add 4–5 tbsp water to soften the ingredients and produce a paste-like texture, then cook for further 4 minutes to thicken.

3 Add the garlic, ginger and chillies and fry (sauté) lightly for 1 minute.

4 Add the salt, turmeric, garam masala and black pepper and cook for 1 minute, stirring to blend the spices together.

5 Add the tomatoes and heat for about 5 minutes until the oil rises to the top and separates from the rest of the ingredients.

6 Remove the pan from the heat and allow to cool for 2 minutes. Mix in the coconut milk and yoghurt and stir thoroughly until both are blended into the rest of the ingredients.

7 Return the pan to the heat, add the fish fillets and stir for 2 minutes over a medium heat, then cover and simmer over a low heat for about 8–10 minutes.

8 Add the lemon and lime juices, garnish with the coriander and serve.

- Serve with Desi Fried Chawal (see page 99), Tarwala Dahi (see page 136) and hot naans.

- You could use a 230 g/8 oz/small can or half a 400 g/14 oz/large can of chopped tomatoes instead of fresh.

Tandoori Machchi

TANDOORI COD STEAKS

This is one for the lads as it is easy to prepare, quick to cook and tastes sensational. Babita's husband often prepares it, then freezes it for when he has a few mates round after a night out – much healthier and tastier than a doner kebab! Try making your own tandoori paste (see page 14) instead of using ready made.

serves 4–6 | preparation 10 minutes | marinating 30 minutes | cooking 20 minutes

6 large cod steaks
3 tbsp tandoori paste
150 ml/¹/₄ pt/small pot of Greek yoghurt
¹/₄ tsp salt

¹/₂ tsp freshly ground black pepper
a handful of chopped fresh coriander
  (cilantro), to garnish

1 Cut three or four slits about 5 cm/2 in deep into both sides of each cod steak.

2 Mix together the tandoori paste, yoghurt, salt and pepper and mix until you get an evenly pink-coloured marinade.

3 Dip each of the cod steaks into the marinade and rub it into the slits.

4 Spoon the remaining marinade over the cod steaks, cover with clingfilm (plastic wrap) and chill for at least 30 minutes before cooking.

5 Cook the steaks on a hot barbecue or under a preheated grill (broiler) for only 6–8 minutes on each side.

6 Garnish with the coriander and serve.

SERVING SUGGESTIONS AND TIPS

- Enjoy with rice, chapattis or naans, salad and Masala Dahi (see page 138).

Shahi Jhinga Masala

KING PRAWN CURRY

Succulent king prawns are here bathed in a rich velvety masala sauce made from a blend of paprika, garlic, cream and chillies enhanced by a zingy lemon and lime flavour. This is certainly a superior dish suitable for a special occasion, yet it's still so quick and easy to prepare.

serves 4–6 | preparation 10 minutes | cooking 25 minutes

25–30 raw unpeeled king tiger prawns
(shrimp)
3 tbsp olive oil
2 onions, chopped
1¹/₂ tsp cumin seeds
4 garlic cloves, crushed
4 cm/1¹/₂ in piece of root ginger, chopped
2 green finger chillies, chopped
¹/₄ tsp salt
¹/₄ tsp freshly ground black pepper

1 tsp turmeric
1¹/₂ tsp garam masala
1¹/₂ tsp paprika
4 tomatoes, chopped
2 tbsp single (light) cream
juice of 1 lemon
juice of 1 lime
lemon wedges and a handful of chopped
fresh coriander (cilantro), to garnish

1   Peel the prawns. Cut down the middle to expose and remove the black vein. Rinse the prawns in cold running water.

2   Heat the oil in a deep saucepan for 1 minute. Add the onions and cook for about 3 minutes over a medium heat until they are soft and translucent.

3   Add the cumin seeds, garlic, ginger and chillies and fry (sauté) lightly for 1 minute.

4   Add the salt, pepper, turmeric, garam masala and paprika and cook for 1 minute until the spices have cooked and blended together.

5   Add the tomatoes and heat for about 5 minutes until the oil rises to the top and separates from the rest of the ingredients.

6   Remove the pan from the heat and allow to cool for 2 minutes, then stir in the cream.

7   Return the pan to the heat, add the prawns and stir for about 8 minutes over a low heat until all the ingredients have blended and the prawns have heated through.

8 Mix in the lemon and lime juices and cook for a further 2 minutes.

9 Garnish with lemon wedges and the coriander and serve.

SERVING SUGGESTIONS AND TIPS

- Serve with Desi Fried Chawal (see page 99), Tarwala Dahi (see page 136) and hot naans.

Bhuna Jhinga Sath Nal Mirch te Dhainya

PAN-FRIED KING PRAWNS WITH GREEN CHILLIES AND CORIANDER

An exotic, sizzling dish vibrant with pink and green colours, the king prawns are covered in a zesty chilli sauce that makes every mouthful an exciting bite! This is another of those fish recipes that combines just a few ingredients to produce a dish that is far more than the sum of its parts.

serves 4–6 | preparation 10 minutes | marinating 20 minutes | cooking 10 minutes

25–30 raw unpeeled king tiger prawns
 (shrimp)
juice of 1 lemon
juice of 1 lime
3 large garlic cloves, crushed
3 green finger chillies, halved lengthways

½ tsp salt
½ tsp freshly ground black pepper
1 tsp cumin seeds
3 tbsp olive oil
a handful of chopped fresh coriander
 (cilantro), to garnish

1 Peel the prawns. Cut down the middle to expose and remove the black vein. Rinse the prawns in cold running water.

2 Pour the lemon and lime juice into a large bowl, add the garlic, chillies, salt, pepper and the prawns and mix together. Cover with clingfilm (plastic wrap) and leave in the fridge to marinate for at least 20 minutes.

3 Dry-fry the cumin seeds in a frying pan (skillet) or wok for 1 minute over a medium heat, then add the oil and heat for 1 minute.

4 Add all of the ingredients from the bowl and fry (sauté) for about 8 minutes over a medium heat, stirring occasionally and ensuring that the prawns turn pink.

5 Garnish with the coriander and a squeeze more lime juice, if liked, and serve.

SERVING SUGGESTIONS

- Enjoy with hot naans and Sona's Desi Salad (see page 29).

Daddiji's Machchi te Matter Sabji

DAD'S FISH AND PEAS

*This is Win's dad's favourite dish that he made when left in charge of the children.
It was usually served with one of his infamous very large fresh chapattis. Using
mainly cupboard ingredients, this recipe takes very little time and effort to prepare.
Deliciously spiced-up pilchards captured in a tomato sauce, Punjabi style.*

serves 4 | preparation 10 minutes | cooking 15 minutes

400 g/14 oz/large can of pilchards in
  tomato sauce
1¹/₂ tsp cumin seeds
4 tbsp olive oil
1 onion, chopped
3 garlic cloves, crushed, or ³/₄ tsp garlic
  paste
4 cm/1¹/₂ in piece of root ginger, grated,
  or ³/₄ tsp ginger paste

1¹/₄ tsp turmeric
1 tsp salt
1¹/₄ tsp tandoori masala
1¹/₄ tsp garam masala
2 green finger chillies, chopped
¹/₂ cup frozen peas
a large handful of chopped fresh
  coriander (cilantro), to garnish

1 Pour the contents of the can of pilchards into a bowl. With a sharp knife, gently
  slice each pilchard lengthways in half to reveal the bones. Scoop out the bones
  with a spoon and discard (don't worry if the pilchards become a little mashed at
  this stage).

2 Dry-fry the cumin seeds for 1 minute over a medium heat, then add the oil, onion,
  garlic and ginger. Cook for about 3–4 minutes, stirring constantly with a wooden
  spoon, until golden brown.

3 Stir in the turmeric, salt, tandoori masala and garam masala and cook for
  2 minutes, stirring occasionally, until the spices are cooked.

4 Add the chillies, stir and cook for a further 2 minutes.

5 Add the pilchards and roughly mix and mash with a wooden spoon.

6 Mix in the peas. Heat through over a low heat for 10 minutes.

7 Garnish with the coriander and serve.

SERVING SUGGESTIONS

• Serve with Khooshboo Elachi Chawal (see page 98), chapattis and Masala Dahi
  (see page 138) or plain yoghurt as an accompaniment.

Masaledar Machchi Curry

MASALA FISH CURRY

Crispy, golden nuggets of white fish pieces coated in chick pea flour and bathed in an exhilarating spicy masala and tomato chunks, this makes a tasty, delicious and tanatalising dish to liven up any dinner party. Just about any white fish will work well in this recipe, but cod is particularly good.

serves 4 | **preparation 10 minutes** | **cooking 15–20 minutes**

2 white fish fillets, cut into bite-sized chunks
6 tbsp chick pea (garbanzo) flour
8–10 tbsp vegetable oil
2 green finger chillies, chopped
3–4 garlic cloves, chopped, or 3/4 tsp garlic paste
4 cm/1 1/2 in piece of root ginger, grated, or 3/4 tsp ginger paste

3 tbsp olive oil
2 curry leaves or 1 tsp medium curry powder
1 tsp carom seeds
1 1/4 tsp salt
3–4 tomatoes, chopped
1 tsp garam masala
a large handful of fresh coriander (cilantro), chopped

1 Coat the fish chunks in the flour.

2 Heat the vegetable oil in a wok, add the fish and fry (sauté) until golden brown. Remove and set aside. Alternatively, you can deep-fry the fish.

3 Whiz together the chillies, garlic and ginger in a blender or grinder to make a paste.

4 Heat the olive oil in a large saucepan over a medium heat, add the curry leaves or powder and carom seeds and heat until the seeds begin to pop. Add the chilli mixture and salt and cook for 3–4 minutes.

5 Add the tomatoes and cook for a further 4–6 minutes until the oil rises to the top.

6 Add the fried fish and garam masala and heat through for 2–3 minutes, then stir in the coriander and serve.

SERVING SUGGESTIONS AND TIPS

- Great with rice, and also naans, chapattis or tortilla wraps, with yoghurt and salad as accompaniments.

- As a variation, substitute prawns, chicken or tofu or paneer cubes for the fish fillets.

- Substitute 3 tbsp rice flour for 3 tbsp of the garbanzo flour for a crisper coating.

SOMETHING MAIN – FISH

Khass Khaney Ki Cheej – Dhals

SOMETHING MAIN – LENTILS

Traditionally Punjabi dhals are slowly cooked inside a clay oven and seasoned simply with tumeric and salt, then left for several hours to create a soupy broth. This is then spiced up with fried tharka seasoning (in the Punjab this is typically a mixture of onions, garlic, ginger and chillies but in other parts of India only fried masala spices) and then served. This is where the term 'tharka dhal' that you'll probably recognise from Indian restaurant menus comes from.

Dhals are delicious, wholesome and nutritious and are great winter warmers. They are generally served with other vegetable, fish or meat curry dishes and breads and rice. You can always adjust the spiciness of your dishes to suit your taste. Use one chilli to give a mild dish, two for medium, three for hot or four for very hot.

Photograph opposite:
**My Friend's Goan Fish Curry (page 66)
with Sona's Indian Salad (page 29).**

Tharka Moong te Masran Di Dhal

SEASONED SPLIT YELLOW AND RED LENTIL DHAL

This is made from dried red lentils (masran di dhal) and split yellow lentils (moong dhal), neither of which require soaking, and creates a delectable, creamy broth. The fried seasoning, or tharka, is based on the Punjabi version that includes garlic and onions. For an authentic flavour, the tharka is best fried in butter.

serves 4–6 | preparation 5 minutes | cooking 40 minutes

For the dhal
$\frac{1}{2}$ **cup dried red lentils, washed in several**
    changes of water
$\frac{1}{2}$ **cup split yellow lentils. washed in**
    several changes of water
5 cups water
1$\frac{1}{2}$ tsp salt
1$\frac{1}{2}$ tsp turmeric
1 tsp butter
2–3 whole green finger chillies

For the tharka
1$\frac{1}{2}$ tsp cumin seeds
4 tbsp butter or olive oil
1 onion, chopped
3–4 garlic cloves, crushed,
    or $\frac{3}{4}$ tsp garlic paste
4 cm/1$\frac{1}{2}$ in piece of root ginger, grated,
    or $\frac{3}{4}$ tsp garlic paste
1$\frac{1}{2}$ tsp garam masala
a large handful of chopped fresh
    coriander (cilantro), to garnish

1 To make the dhal, place the washed lentils in a large saucepan. Add the water, salt, turmeric, butter and whole chillies.

2 Bring to the boil, cover and lower the heat. Simmer for about 30–35 minutes, stirring occasionally, until the dhal is a pourable, not too thick, consistency. If it over-thickens, add some boiled water to get it to the right consistency and cook for about 5 minutes.

3 Meanwhile, to make the tharka, dry-roast the cumin seeds in a frying pan (skillet) over a medium heat. Add the butter or oil, heat for 1 minute, then add the onion, garlic and ginger and cook for about 5–6 minutes until golden brown. Add the tharka to the dhal and mix.

4 Remove the saucepan from the heat and add the garam masala.

5 Garnish with the coriander and serve.

Photograph opposite:
Masala Roast Chicken Pieces (page 91)
with Aromatic Cardamom Rice (page 98).

Lazeez Panch Puran Dhal

DELICIOUS FIVE LENTIL DHAL

Mixed dhals usually consist of two or three different types of lentil. This recipe is a little different in that it uses a variety of coloured lentils, creating a delicious mixed dish. The various beans and lentils provide a nutritious source of protein and the end result is a wholesome, bean-like, spicy broth with a bite.

serves 4–6 | preparation 10 minutes | cooking 1¹/₂ hours

For the dhal
¹/₄ **cup spilt yellow lentils**
¹/₄ **cup green lentils**
¹/₄ **cup brown lentils**
¹/₄ **cup black lentils**
3 **tbsp dried kidney beans**
9 **cups water**
1¹/₂ **tsp salt**
1¹/₂ **tsp turmeric**
1 **tsp butter**
2–3 **whole green finger chillies**

For the tharka
4–5 **tbsp butter or olive oil**
1 **large onion, chopped**
3–4 **garlic cloves, crushed, or** ³/₄ **tsp garlic paste**
4 **cm/1¹/₂ in piece of root ginger, grated, or** ³/₄ **tsp garlic paste**
1¹/₂ **tsp garam masala**
a large handful of chopped fresh coriander (cilantro), to garnish

1 To make the dhal, place all the lentils and the kidney beans in a large saucepan and wash in several changes of water.

2 Add the water, salt, turmeric, butter and whole chillies, bring to boil, part-cover and lower the heat. Simmer for about 1¹/₄ hours, stirring every 10 minutes, until the lentils soften. If they are not soft by the end of this time, add ¹/₂ cup more water and continue to simmer for a further 15 minutes.

3 Meanwhile, to make the tharka, heat the butter or olive oil in a frying pan (skillet). Add the onion, garlic and ginger and cook for about 5–6 minutes until golden brown. Add the tharka to the dhal and mix. Stir in the garam masala, garnish with the coriander and serve.

SERVING SUGGESTIONS AND TIPS

- Serve with chapattis or rice.
- An alternative, sweeter tharka can be made with 4 cm/1¹/₂ in piece of root ginger, grated, 1 tbsp cumin seeds, ¹/₂ tsp hot chilli powder and 1¹/₂ tsp garam masala. Cook as at step 3. This can be used in any of the dhal recipes.

Desi Tari Wale Kaley Chole

INDIAN BLACK CHICK PEA CURRY

Wholesome and nutty in taste, black chick peas are a little harder in texture and more strongly flavoured then normal chick peas – definitely worth a try. In this recipe, which we learned from Win's mum, they are bathed in a tantalising spicy masala sauce thickened with potato.

serves 4–6 | preparation 10 minutes | cooking 35–40 minutes

1 large baking potato

1¹/₂ tsp cumin seeds

4 tbsp olive oil

1 large onion, finely chopped

4 garlic cloves, crushed, or ³/₄ tsp garlic paste

4 cm/1¹/₂ in piece root ginger, grated, or ³/₄ tsp ginger paste

1¹/₂ tsp salt

1 tsp turmeric

1¹/₂ tsp tandoori masala

3 tomatoes, finely chopped

2 green finger chillies, finely chopped

400 g/14 oz/large can of black chick peas (garbanzos), drained and rinsed

2 cups water

1¹/₂ tsp garam masala

a large handful of fresh coriander (cilantro), chopped

1 Microwave the potato for about 8 minutes on High until cooked. When cool enough to handle, scoop out the insides and mash roughly with a fork. Set aside.

2 Dry-roast the cumin seeds in a large saucepan over a medium heat until they begin to pop. Add the oil and onion and cook for 2 minutes, then add the garlic and ginger and cook for about 3–4 minutes, stirring occasionally, until golden brown.

3 Add the salt, turmeric and tandoori masala and cook for 1 minute, stirring. Add the tomatoes and chillies. Stir frequently to obtain a smooth paste, then cook until the oil rises to the top and separates from the paste.

4 Add the chick peas and cook for 5 minutes.

5 Add the water and bring to the boil, then cover and cook for 20 minutes.

6 Add the mashed potato to thicken the sauce and cook for a further 5 minutes.

7 Remove from the heat, add the garam masala and coriander and serve.

SERVING SUGGESTIONS AND TIPS

- Serve with hot chapattis, naans, pooris, Dahi Wale Bhaturey (see page 111) or rice and Masala Dahi (see page 138) as an accompaniment.

Mum Deh Lazeez Rajma

RED KIDNEY BEAN CURRY

*This is Babita's all-time favourite vegetarian dish. It's her mum's famous recipe,
which uses delicious red kidney beans covered in a luscious spicy tomato curry sauce.
You have to taste it to believe it! Babita likes it medium-hot so we use two chillies;
you can make it milder or hotter if you prefer.*

serves 4–6 | preparation 10 minutes | cooking 40 minutes

4 tbsp olive oil
1 tsp cumin seeds
2 onions, chopped
3 garlic cloves, crushed
5 cm/2 in piece of root ginger, chopped
2 green finger chillies, chopped
4 tomatoes, chopped
1¹/₂ tsp salt
1¹/₂ tsp turmeric

1 tsp paprika
1¹/₂ tsp curry powder
1¹/₂ tsp garam masala
600 g/1 lb 6 oz/1¹/₂ large cans of red
 kidney beans, drained and rinsed
1¹/₂ cup water
a handful of fresh coriander (cilantro),
 chopped

1 Heat the oil in a large saucepan for 2 minutes. Add the cumin seeds and listen for them to start popping (this will take about 1–2 minutes).

2 Add the onions and cook for about 3 minutes over a medium heat until they are soft and translucent.

3 Add the garlic, ginger and chillies and fry (sauté) gently over a medium heat for about 2 minutes.

4 Add 4–5 tbsp of water to make the ingredients softer and paste-like. Cook for further 4 minutes.

5 Add the tomatoes and heat for about 5 minutes until the oil rises to the top and separates from the rest of the ingredients.

6 Add the salt, turmeric, paprika, curry powder and garam masala and cook for 2 minutes until the spices have cooked and blended together.

7 Add the kidney beans and stir through for 2 minutes until blended.

8 Add the water and bring to the boil. Reduce the heat, cover and simmer for about 20–25 minutes until the red kidney beans are cooked through.

9 Stir in the coriander and serve.

- Enjoy this dish with rice of your choice, Masala Dahi (see page 138) and Sona's Desi Salad (see page 29).

Sukhe Urid Dhal

DRIED SPLIT WHITE LENTIL DHAL

This is another of Babita's mum's inventions. Normally dhal has a soupy consistency; this alternative way to cook it results in a drier dish, full of flavour and with a velvety texture and golden colour. Use two chillies for a medium dish but add one or two more if you like your food a bit hotter.

serves 4–6 | preparation 5 minutes | cooking 35 minutes

1 cup dried split white lentils, washed in several changes of water

3 tbsp olive oil

1 tsp cumin seeds

1 onion, thinly sliced

4 garlic cloves, chopped

5 cm/2 in piece of ginger, grated

2 small green finger chillies, chopped

1¼ tsp turmeric (optional)

1 tsp salt

½ tsp freshly ground black pepper

a handful of fresh coriander (cilantro), chopped

1 Place the washed lentils in a large saucepan of water and bring to the boil. Simmer for 15 minutes, then remove, drain and set aside.

2 Heat the oil in another large saucepan for 2 minutes. Add the cumin seeds and listen for them to start popping (this will take about 1–2 minutes).

3 Add the onion and cook for about 3 minutes over a medium heat until they are soft and translucent.

4 Add the garlic, ginger, chillies and turmeric, if using, and fry gently for about 2 minutes.

5 Stir the lentils into the saucepan, then add the salt and pepper and cook for about 2 minutes until the spices have cooked and blended together.

6 Reduce the heat, cover and simmer for 15–20 minutes, stirring frequently, until the dhal is cooked through.

7 Stir in the coriander and serve.

SERVING SUGGESTIONS AND TIPS

- Serve with simple chapattis, a yoghurt dish and Gajar Ka Achar (see page 137).

Khass Khaney Ki Cheej – Gosht

SOMETHING MAIN – MEAT

Meat dishes are popular in Northern India, especially in the Punjab where mutton and lamb (bakra) are cooked dry or wet, and fresh organic chicken (murgi) is often cooked in a tomato-based sauce with spices and served for a special occasions.

Traditionally beef is not eaten in India because cows are seen as sacred in the Hindu and Sikh religions. From our research, pork is eaten by non-Muslims, especially in southern parts of India such as Goa, so we've included a pork recipe. Most of our dishes, though are based on chicken and lamb. In our households 'Chak De Phate' Murgi (Kickin' Chicken Curry, see page 88) is a firm Saturday night favourite, as is Keema te Matter (Minced Lamb and Peas, see page 80) served with chapattis and rice, raita and salad. Jas's Sukha Mutton (Jas's Dry Lamb Curry, see page 83) is popular by itself – a great one for a boys' night in with a shot or two of alcohol!

Sabh Ki Pasand Mutton Curry

EVERYONE'S FAVOURITE LAMB CURRY

A must for meat eaters and very addictive. Velvety chunks of succulent lamb are here blended and cooked in garlic, ginger and flavoursome masala spices topped with fresh coriander to create an enticing meat dish. Another Saturday night favourite!

serves 4–6 | preparation 10 minutes | cooking 55 minutes

4 tbsp olive oil

2 onions, chopped

3–4 garlic cloves, crushed, or ³/₄ tsp garlic paste

4 cm/1¹/₂ in piece of root ginger, chopped, or ³/₄ tsp ginger paste

2–4 green finger chillies, chopped

1¹/₂ tsp salt

1¹/₂ tsp turmeric

2 tsp tandoori masala

1¹/₂ tsp Madras curry paste (optional)

4 tomatoes, chopped

450 g/1 lb diced lamb

2 cups water

1¹/₂ tsp garam masala

a handful of fresh coriander (cilantro), chopped

1 Heat the oil in a saucepan or wok for 2 minutes. Add the onions and cook for about 3–4 minutes over a medium heat until they are soft and translucent.

2 Add the garlic, ginger and chillies and fry (sauté) lightly for 2 minutes.

3 Add the salt, turmeric, tandoori masala and Madras curry paste, if using, and cook for 1 minute until the spices have cooked and blended together.

4 Add the tomatoes and stir frequently to blend to a smooth paste. Cook for about 5 minutes until the oil separates from the paste and rises to the top.

5 Add the lamb and heat and stir through for 2 minutes until blended.

6 Add the water and bring to the boil. Reduce the heat, cover and simmer for 50 minutes until the water has reduced to a sauce.

7 Stir in the garam masala and coriander and serve.

SERVING SUGGESTIONS AND TIPS

- Enjoy this dish with chapattis, crispy flat breads, naans, tortilla wraps or rice, and a yoghurt accompaniment.

- For a drier curry, add only ³/₄ cup of water, or for a creamier sauce, add yoghurt.

Keema te Matter

MINCED LAMB AND PEAS

A brilliant Saturday night dish in our homes, and one we both grew up on, this is made with succulent lamb mince sweated with onions, garlic and ginger and combined with juicy tomatoes and tanatalising masala spices to create a mouth-watering meaty dish. Kidneys can be added as an extra ingredient if you like.

serves 4–6 | **preparation 15 minutes** | **cooking 50 minutes**

1 tbsp cumin seeds
4 tbsp olive oil
2 onions, chopped
3 garlic cloves, crushed
4 cm/1½ in piece of root ginger, grated
1¼ tsp salt
1½ tsp turmeric
1½ tsp tandoori masala
2 green finger chillies, finely chopped

4 tomatoes, chopped
550–700 g/1¼ lb–1½ lb lamb mince
¾ cup lambs' kidney, chopped (optional)
1½ cup water
1 cup peas, defrosted if frozen
1½ tsp garam masala
a large handful of fresh coriander
  (cilantro), chopped

1 Dry-roast the cumin seeds in a saucepan until they begin to pop. Add the oil and onion and fry (sauté) for 1 minute.

2 Add the garlic and ginger and fry for a few minutes until golden brown.

3 Add the salt, turmeric, tandoori masala and chillies and cook for 1 minute.

4 Add the tomatoes and blend to a smooth paste. Cook for about 5 minutes until the oil separates from the paste and rises to the top.

5 Add the mince and kidneys, if using, and mix well. Add the water. Cover and cook over a medium heat for 10 minutes, then lower the heat and cook for a further 25 minutes.

6 Once cooked and most of the water has been absorbed, add the peas and cook for a further 10–15 minutes both peas and meat are cooked through.

7 Stir in the garam masala and coriander and serve.

SERVING SUGGESTIONS AND TIPS

- Enjoy this dish with rice, chapattis, tortilla wraps or pittas, with yoghurt and salad as accompaniments.

- Win's husband, Jas, has his own version of mince and peas, which is a definite hit! He omits the tomatoes and the water, but uses three onions instead of one. He adds the meat with the garlic and ginger, letting it sweat for 10 minutes before adding the salt and spices. He cooks it for a further 25 minutes.

- As a variation, try using pork or chicken mince.

- You could use a 400 g/14 oz/large can of chopped tomatoes instead of fresh.

Bakra Chops

LAMB CHOPS

*A tempting, tantalising dish and one that Babita's brother always comes home for!
Although it has quite a few ingredients, don't be put off as it is really easy to make
and can be left to cook by itself, simmering gently away and filling the kitchen with
delicious, spicy aromas.*

serves 4–6 | preparation 10 minutes | cooking 1 hour

5 tbsp olive oil
1 tsp cumin seeds
4 or 5 whole cloves
2 onions, chopped
5 garlic cloves, crushed
7.5 cm/3 in piece of root ginger, chopped
3 green finger chillies, chopped
4 medium tomatoes, skinned and
   chopped

1¹/₂ tsp salt
1¹/₂ tsp turmeric
1¹/₂ tsp paprika
1¹/₂ tsp curry powder
1¹/₂ tsp garam masala
8–10 lamb chops
1¹/₂ cups water
a handful of fresh coriander (cilantro),
   chopped

1 Heat the oil in a saucepan for 2 minutes, then add the cumin seeds and cloves
   and fry (sauté) for about 2 minutes until the cumin seeds start popping.

2 Add the onions, garlic, ginger and chillies and fry gently over a medium heat for
   3 minutes until golden brown.

3 Add 4–5 tbsp of water to make the ingredients softer and form a paste. Cook for a
   further 4 minutes.

4 Add the tomatoes and heat through for about 5 minutes until the oil rises to the
   top and separates from the rest of the ingredients.

5 Add the salt, turmeric, paprika, curry powder and garam masala and cook for
   2 minutes until the spices have cooked and blended together.

6 Add the lamb chops and heat through for 2 minutes, stirring until all the
   ingredients are well blended.

7 Add the water and bring to the boil. Reduce the heat, cover and simmer for about
   40 minutes until the lamb is tender.

8 Add the coriander and serve.

- Enjoy this dish with Desi Fried Chawal (see page 99), Masala Dahi (see page 138), Krishna Ji's Tandoori Roti (see page 102) and Nimbu Ka Achar (see page 140).

Jas's Sukha Mutton

JAS'S DRY LAMB CURRY

Created by Win's husband Jas – juicy chunks of succulent lamb intermingled with garlic, ginger and simple yet flavoursome masala spices create an enticing meat dish. Definitely one for the boys to make and eat on its own or with a shot of alcohol as part of a Saturday night meal.

serves 4–6 | preparation 10 minutes | cooking 45 minutes

4 tbsp olive oil
4 large onions, chopped
3–4 garlic cloves, crushed, or $^3/_4$ tsp garlic paste
4 cm/1$^1/_2$ in piece of root ginger, grated, or $^3/_4$ tsp ginger paste
2–4 green finger chillies, chopped

450 g/1 lb diced lamb
1$^1/_2$ tsp turmeric
1$^1/_2$ tsp garam masala
1$^1/_2$ tsp salt
a handful of fresh coriander (cilantro), chopped

1 Heat the oil in a saucepan or wok for 2 minutes. Add the onions and cook for about 4 minutes over a medium heat until they are soft and translucent.

2 Add the garlic, ginger and chillies and fry (sauté) until browned.

3 Add the lamb and heat and stir through for 5–8 minutes

4 Add the turmeric and garam masala and cook for 5 minutes until the spices have cooked and blended together.

5 Add the salt and stir until it is fully saturated into the ingredients. Reduce the heat and simmer for 25–30 minutes until the lamb is tender, stirring only occasionally so as not to break up the meat.

6 Stir in the coriander and serve.

SERVING SUGGESTIONS AND TIPS

- Enjoy with chappatis, naans, pooris, tortilla wraps or rice.

83

Punjabi Keema Kofte

PUNJABI MINCED MEAT KOFTAS

Luscious minced lamb meatballs are here mingled Punjabi-style with garlic, ginger and tandoori spices. Rolled in rice flour for crispiness, these are delicious served as a snack or as part of a main meal in hot wraps or naans and are really easy to make. Use one chilli for mild koftas, or add more if you wish.

serves 4–6 | preparation 15 minutes | cooking 40 minutes

For the kofte
550–700 g/1¼–1½ lb lamb mince
3–4 garlic cloves, crushed, or ¾ tsp garlic paste
3 cm/1¼ in piece of root ginger, grated, or ¾ tsp ginger paste
a handful of fresh coriander (cilantro), chopped
1½ tsp garam masala
1 tsp salt
1 green finger chilli, finely chopped
5 tbsp rice flour
10 tbsp vegetable or olive oil
For the sauce
1¼ tsp cumin seeds

4 tbsp olive oil
2 onions, finely chopped
3–4 garlic cloves, crushed, or ¾ tsp garlic paste
4 cm/1½ in piece of root ginger, grated, or ¾ tsp ginger paste
1¼ tsp turmeric
1 tsp salt
1¼ tsp tandoori masala
3 large tomatoes fresh chopped
1–2 green finger chillies, finely chopped
1 cup water
1¼ tsp garam masala
a large handful of chopped fresh coriander, to garnish

1 To make the kofte, blend together all the ingredients except the oil. Shape into clementine-sized balls.

2 Heat the oil in a frying pan (skillet) and fry (sauté) the balls until browned all over. Remove and set aside.

3 To make the sauce, dry-roast the cumin seeds in a large frying pan for about 2 minutes until they start popping.

4 Add the oil and fry the onions, garlic and ginger until lightly browned.

5 Stir in the turmeric, salt, tandoori masala, tomatoes and chillies. Cook over a low heat, blending and stirring with a wooden spoon or potato masher, until a smooth paste is formed and the oil rises to the top.

6 Add the water and simmer for 15 minutes to blend the spices.

7 Add the kofte and cook for about 25 minutes until they are cooked through and a thick sauce has formed. Stir in the garam masala.

8 Remove from the heat, garnish with the coriander and serve.

SERVING SUGGESTIONS AND TIPS

- Enjoy this dish with naans, chapattis, tortilla wraps, pittas or rice.
- For a vegetarian alternative, see our Soya Kofte (page 60).

Dahi Gosht Kebab

YOGHURT PORK KEBAB

A great barbecue dish, the chunks of pork are bathed in a creamy yoghurt marinade, while the fennel adds as an excellent aniseed taste that complements the pork wonderfully. As a variation, use chicken or lamb chunks, or try it made with uncooked paneer chunks, but omit the fennel for that dish.

serves 4–6 | preparation 5 minutes | marinating 25 minutes | cooking 10 minutes

450 g/1 lb diced pork
1 green (bell) pepper, cut into small pieces
1 red pepper, cut into small pieces
150 ml/¼ pt/small pot of plain yoghurt
½ tsp salt
1 tsp fennel seeds

1 tsp Madras curry paste
1 tsp tandoori masala
1 tsp garam masala
2–3 green finger chillies, chopped
2 bay leaves
a large handful of chopped fresh coriander (cilantro), to garnish

1 Thread the pork and pepper pieces on to soaked wooden barbecue skewers.

2 Mix together the yoghurt, salt, spices and chillies in a baking dish. Add the kebabs and turn in the marinade to bathe completely. Leave to marinate in the fridge for 25 minutes.

3 Barbecue for 6–8 minutes, turning until cooked.

4 Garnish with the coriander and serve.

SERVING SUGGESTIONS AND TIPS

- Enjoy this dish with rice or roll up in chapattis, tortilla wraps or pitta bread, with yoghurt and salad as accompaniments.

- You could also cook the kebabs under a hot grill (broiler) instead of barbecuing.

- Instead of making kebabs, fry (sauté) together all the spices and paste except the garam masala in 4 tbsp of oil. Add the yoghurt, vegetables, 1 cup of water and the pork and cook for 25 minutes until the pork is cooked through. Finally, add the garam masala and garnish with coriander. Serve with the suggestions above.

Jaldi Masaledar Murgi

SPEEDY MASALA CHICKEN STRIPS

A recipe that's very popular with Win's brother. It's just as quick to prepare as it is to eat, there's very little chopping – you just chuck it in. A great one for the boys – and girls – to make before footie on the box or after a night out. The full flavours of the spices come together, complemented by the tomatoes, to make a lip-smacking dish.

serves 4–6 | preparation 5 minutes | cooking 15 minutes

1 tsp cumin seeds
4 tbsp olive oil
1½ tsp turmeric
¾ tsp salt
¾ tsp Madras curry paste (optional)
2 green finger chillies, chopped
450 g/1 lb stir-fry chicken strips

1 large tomato, chopped
3 tbsp water
1¼ tsp garam masala
a large handful of fresh coriander
  (cilantro), chopped
2 tbsp dried fenugreek leaves (optional)

1 Dry-roast the cumin seeds in a large frying pan (skillet) or wok for 1 minute.

2 Add the oil and when heated stir in the turmeric, salt, Madras curry paste, if using, and chillies. Stir for 1 minute.

3 Add the chicken strips and lightly brown for 5 minutes, stirring frequently.

4 Stir in the the tomato and water. Cook for 6–8 minutes, stirring frequently with a wooden spoon to soften the tomato.

5 Remove from the heat. Stir in the garam masala, coriander and fenugreek, if using, mix together and serve.

SERVING SUGGESTIONS AND TIPS

- Serve in naans, chapattis, pittas or tortilla wraps, drizzle with yoghurt and serve with a salad.

- As a variation, stir in 1½–2 tbsp plain yoghurt for a creamy sauce or flavour with 1½ tsp creamed coconut with the coriander.

'Chak De Phate' Murgi

KICKIN' CHICKEN CURRY

*The famously irresistible chicken curry made within most Punjabi households –
delicious, addictive and explosive! Just add family or friends and tuck in. Our friend
Keith loves this recipe and has even served it up with traditional roasted vegetables
on a Sunday and on hot toast.*

serves 4–6 | preparation 10 minutes | cooking 50 minutes

4 tbsp olive oil

2 onions, chopped

3–4 garlic cloves, chopped, or ³/₄ tsp garlic paste

4 cm/1¹/₂ in piece of root ginger, chopped, or ³/₄ tsp ginger paste

1¹/₂ tsp salt

1¹/₂ tsp turmeric

1¹/₂ tsp Madras curry paste (optional)

1¹/₂ tsp tandoori masala

2–4 green finger chillies, chopped

4 tomatoes, chopped

8–10 skinless chicken pieces (thighs, drumsticks, etc.)

2 cups water

1¹/₂ tsp garam masala

a handful of fresh coriander (cilantro), chopped

1 Heat the oil in a saucepan or wok for 2 minutes. Add the onions and cook for about 4 minutes over a medium heat until they are soft and translucent.

2 Add the garlic and ginger and fry (sauté) lightly for 2 minutes.

3 Add the salt, turmeric, Madras curry paste, if using, and tandoori masala and cook for 1 minute until the spices have cooked and blended together.

4 Add the chillies and tomatoes and heat for about 5 minutes until the oil rises to the top and separates from the rest of the ingredients.

5 Add the chicken and heat and stir through for 2 minutes until all the ingredients have blended.

6 Add the water and bring to the boil. Reduce the heat, cover and simmer for 40 minutes until the water has reduced to a sauce.

7 Stir in the garam masala and coriander and serve.

SERVING SUGGESTIONS AND TIPS

- Enjoy this dish with chapattis, crispy flat breads, naans, tortilla wraps or rice and a yoghurt accompaniment.

- If you're in a hurry, use chicken breast meat chopped into 5 cm/2 in cubes and cook for 20 minutes only.

- For a drier curry, add only $^3/_4$ cup of water.

- For a creamier sauce, stir in 2 tbsp of yoghurt with the garam masala.

- A friend of ours cooks this dish in a different way: omit the tomatoes and water and add the salt with the chicken to make it sweat in its juices. This makes a tempting, juicy dish that resembles Jas's Sukha Mutton (see page 93).

- You could use a 400 g/14 oz/large can of chopped tomatoes instead of fresh.

Jaldi Murgi Palak

QUICK CHICKEN AND SPINACH

A fantastic combination of spicy chicken and nutritious, vibrant greens, this makes an ideal dish to impress your family and friends. The spinach brings the dish alive, creating a colourful, mouth-watering, enticing yet healthy dish that's great for supper or for a dinner party.

serves 4–6 | **preparation 5 minutes** | **cooking 15 minutes**

³/₄ tsp cumin seeds
4 tbsp olive oil
1 large onion, chopped
3 garlic cloves, crushed,
  or ³/₄ tsp garlic paste
4 cm/1¹/₂ in piece of root ginger, grated,
  or ³/₄ tsp ginger paste
1 tsp turmeric
³/₄ tsp salt

2 green finger chillies, chopped
450 g/1 lb stir-fry chicken strips or
  chicken breast, cubed
300 g/11 oz/large bag of baby spinach
  leaves
1¹/₄ tsp garam masala
a handful of fresh coriander (cilantro),
  chopped

1 Dry-roast the cumin seeds in a large frying pan (skillet) or wok for 1 minute.

2 Add the oil and onion and fry (sauté) for 3 minutes, stirring occasionally.

3 Add the garlic, ginger, turmeric, salt and chillies and fry for 2 minutes.

4 Add the chicken strips and lightly brown for 5 minutes, stirring frequently.

5 Add the spinach and cook for a further 8–10 minutes until it has wilted and the chicken is cooked through.

6 Remove from the heat. Stir in the garam masala and coriander and serve.

SERVING SUGGESTIONS AND TIPS

- Serve with rice, chapattis or naans and Masala Dahi (see page 138).

- As a variation, other types of meat can be substituted for the chicken. For a vegetarian alternative, use fried paneer cubes (see page 16) instead of the chicken.

Masaledar Bhuna Murgi

MASALA ROAST CHICKEN PIECES

*A quick and easy dish, this is a definite way to liven up good old roast chicken
or chicken pieces. They are tossed in a wonderful array of colourful, exciting spices
and combined with juicy tomatoes and pepper strips, then finished off with fresh
green coriander.*

serves 4 | preparation 10 minutes | cooking 20 minutes

2 tbsp cumin seeds
1 tbsp black mustard seeds (optional)
4 tbsp olive oil
3 garlic cloves, crushed
4 cm/1½ in piece of root ginger, grated
2 green finger chillies, chopped
1 tsp salt
1¼ tsp tandoori masala
1¼ tsp garam masala

3 large tomatoes, chopped
1 large red or green (bell) pepper, cut into
  strips
8 ready-roasted chicken pieces (thighs,
  drumsticks etc.)
1 large handful of fresh coriander,
  chopped
2 tbsp dried fenugreek leaves (optional)

1 Dry-roast the cumin seeds and mustard seeds, if using, in a wok over a medium
   heat until they begin to pop.

2 Add the oil and when hot stir in the garlic, ginger, chillies, salt, tandoori masala
   and garam masala.

3 Add the tomatoes and pepper strips and fry (sauté) for 5–6 minutes until soft.

4 Add the chicken and heat, stirring occasionally, until heated through.

5 Add the coriander and fenugreek, if using, and serve.

SERVING SUGGESTIONS AND TIPS

- If you have time, you could ready-roast the uncooked chicken pieces for this
  recipe yourself at 190°C/375°F/gas 5/fan oven 170°C for 40–45 minutes.

- Enjoy this dish with mashed potato or rice and serve with yoghurt and salad.

- As a variation, add 1 tbsp each of yoghurt and single cream for a creamy sauce.

- You can make a vegetarian alternative to this by using fried paneer cubes
  (see page 16).

Tharka Murgi

SEASONED CHICKEN

A great dish created by one of our single male friends who loves to cook traditional Indian food quickly and in one pot, this offers tempting, spicy chicken in a creamy yoghurt sauce. Although marinated for a much shorter time than for typical traditional dishes, the spices seep into the chicken to create a scrumptious dish.

serves 4 | preparation 10 minutes | marinating 30 minutes | cooking 30 minutes

150 ml/¹/₄ pt/small pot of plain yoghurt
1¹/₂ tsp tandoori masala
1¹/₂ tsp ground coriander (cilantro)
1¹/₂ tsp ground cumin
1¹/₂ tsp chicken seasoning or masala
6–8 skinless chicken pieces (thighs, etc.)
4 tbsp sunflower or olive oil
4 garlic cloves, crushed, or ³/₄ tsp garlic paste

4 cm/1¹/₂ in piece of root ginger, thinly sliced lengthways, or ³/₄ tsp ginger paste
2 onions, chopped
2–4 green finger chillies, chopped
1¹/₂ tsp salt
a handful of chopped fresh coriander, to garnish

1 Mix together the yoghurt, tandoori masala, ground coriander, cumin and chicken seasoning or masala. Add the chicken pieces and leave for 30 minutes to marinate.

2 Heat the oil in a non-stick wok and add the garlic and ginger. Fry (sauté) for about 4 minutes until lightly browned.

3 Lift the chicken out of the marinade, add to the wok and stir-fry for about 12–15 minutes until evenly browned.

4 Remove everything from the wok and set aside. Add the onions, chillies and salt and fry for about 4 minutes until golden-brown.

5 Add the remaining marinade to the wok and cook for 5 minutes.

6 Return the reserved ingredients to the wok and cook for 10 minutes until heated through.

7 Garnish with the fresh coriander and serve.

SERVING SUGGESTIONS AND TIPS

- Enjoy this dish with naans, tortilla wraps or rice, with a yoghurt accompaniment.

Khatta Mitha Murgi Tikka Masala

TANGY CHICKEN CURRY

A tangy and creamy variation on chicken curry and a recipe that we've both cooked many times for dinner parties, with great success. The sherry imparts a yummy sweetness, coupled with the creamy yoghurt and coconut flavours just grabbing those taste buds.

serves 4–6 | preparation 10 minutes | cooking 50 minutes

4 tbsp olive oil

2 onions, chopped

3–4 garlic cloves, crushed, or ³/₄ tsp garlic paste

4 cm/1¹/₂ in piece of root ginger, chopped, or ³/₄ tsp ginger paste

2–4 green finger chillies

1¹/₂ tsp salt

1¹/₂ tsp turmeric

1¹/₂ tsp medium curry powder

4 tomatoes, chopped

700–900 g/1¹/₂–2 lb skinless chicken pieces (thighs, drumsticks, etc.)

1 cup water

³/₄ cup dry cooking sherry

1¹/₂ tsp garam masala

2 tbsp creamed coconut

1¹/₂ tbsp yoghurt

1¹/₂ tbsp single (light) cream

a handful of fresh coriander (cilantro), chopped

1 Heat the oil in a saucepan or wok for 2 minutes. Add the onions and cook for about 4 minutes over a medium heat until they are soft and translucent.

2 Add the garlic, ginger and chillies and fry (sauté) lightly for 2 minutes.

3 Add the salt, turmeric and curry powder and cook for 1 minute until the spices have cooked and blended together.

4 Add the tomatoes and heat for about 5 minutes until the oil rises to the top and separates from the rest of the ingredients.

5 Add the chicken pieces and stir for 2 minutes to blend with the other ingredients. Add the water and sherry and bring to the boil. Reduce the heat, cover and simmer for 40 minutes until the liquid has reduced to a sauce.

6 Mix in the garam masala, creamed coconut, yoghurt and cream. Heat through but do not allow to boil. Stir in the coriander and serve.

SERVING SUGGESTIONS AND TIPS

• Enjoy this dish with chapattis, naans, tortilla wraps or rice and a yoghurt dish.

Chawal

RICE

Rice is a versatile component in Indian cuisine in that it can be served simply plain, delicately seasoned with aromatic spices, or cooked with vegetables or meat to create a complete dish of tempting biryani or pilau.

Most Indians use basmati rice, grown in Northern India and Pakistan, which has very white, aromatic and fragrant grains. No wonder it's called 'the queen of rice'! For a healthier option, brown basmati rice is also available but it needs to be cooked for longer.

Ideally, rice should be cooked slightly underdone and left to finish off by itself to keep the grains whole. A few drops of lemon juice or a little butter or ghee (which gives a better flavour than oil) can be added to the cooked rice to ensure the grains stay separate.

Rice is also the foundation for some sweet dishes and desserts, such as Khooshboo Dar Kheer (Aromatic Rice Pudding, see page 119).

Murgi Biryani

CHICKEN AND RICE

Biryanis are technically layered dishes of meat or vegetables and plain or coloured rice. This recipe is for a one-pan biryani and incorporates tasty, meaty chicken pieces combined with rice and flavoured with delectable spices. It comes from one of our bachelor friends, Ravi, who cooks this when in a hurry.

serves 4–6 | preparation 10 minutes | cooking 20 minutes

1 tbsp cumin seeds
2 tbsp black mustard seeds (optional
4 tbsp olive oil
1 onion, chopped
3 garlic cloves, crushed, or $^3/_4$ tsp garlic
   paste
4 cm/$1^1/_2$ in piece of root ginger, grated,
   or $^3/_4$ tsp ginger paste
$^1/_2$ tsp hot chilli powder

$1^1/_4$ tsp salt
$1^1/_4$ tsp chicken masala
2 chicken breasts, cut into bite-sized
   pieces
$1^1/_2$ cups long-grain rice, washed
3 cups water
a handful of chopped fresh coriander
   (cilantro), to garnish

1 Dry-fry the cumin seeds and mustard seeds, if using, in a wok over a medium heat until they begin to pop.

2 Add the oil, and when hot stir in the onion, garlic, ginger, chilli powder, salt and chicken masala. Add the chicken and fry (sauté) for 3 minutes.

3 Add the rice, stir a few times, then add the water. Bring to the boil, then reduce the heat and simmer for about 15 minutes until the rice and chicken are cooked.

4 Garnish with the coriander and serve.

SERVING SUGGESTIONS AND TIPS

- Enjoy this dish with a vegetable curry, yoghurt and a salad.
- To vary this dish, omit the chicken and add mixed vegetables of your choice for a simple Vegetable Biryani, or add fried paneer cubes (see page 16) for Paneer Biryani.

Sabji Biryani

MIXED VEGETABLE RICE

A quick and simple dish commonly used to finish off all those leftover vegetables from the night before. You don't have to stick to the veggies we've suggested – be inventive! This is a great accompaniment to just about any curry, but it's hearty and flavouresome enough to be a complete meal in itself.

serves 4–6 | preparation 5 minutes | cooking 20 minutes

2 tbsp olive oil
1 tsp cumin seeds
1 onion, finely sliced
1 medium potato, cut into 2 cm/^{3}/$_4$ in cubes
a handful of okra (ladies' fingers)
a handful of sweetcorn (corn), fresh or
    frozen
a handful of peas, fresh or frozen

1 carrot, finely sliced
a handful of mushrooms, sliced
1^1/$_2$ cups basmati rice, washed several
    times
1^1/$_4$ tsp salt
1^1/$_2$ tsp garam masala
1^1/$_2$ tsp paprika
3 cups water

1 Heat the oil in a saucepan for 1 minute, then add the cumin seeds and wait for about 1–2 until they start popping.

2 Add the onion and fry (sauté) gently for 2 minutes over a medium heat until it is soft and translucent.

3 Add the potato and cook for 3 minutes, then add the okra, sweetcorn, peas, carrot and mushrooms.

4 Add the rice, salt, garam masala and paprika and stir well to coat the rice grains and vegetables in the spices.

5 Add the water, bring to the boil, then reduce the heat and simmer for about 12–14 minutes.

6 Remove from the heat and stand for 5 minutes to finish cooking before serving.

SERVING SUGGESTIONS AND TIPS

- Enjoy with one of our yoghurt dishes and pickles.

- Use up all of your vegetables that you have in stock, cooked or uncooked.

**Photograph opposite:
Red Kidney Bean Curry (page 76) with Deep-fried
Bread Rounds (page 107) and plain rice.**

Matter Chawal

PEAS AND RICE

This is always popular with Babita's young son and her nieces and nephews, because it's so simply flavoured with cumin seeds and is very easy to eat. It's such a good introduction to the flavours of Indian cooking and it's a great accompaniment for any meat, fish or vegetable curries.

serves 4–6 | preparation 5 minutes | cooking 15 minutes

2 tbsp olive oil
1/2 tsp cumin seeds
1 onion, finely sliced
1 1/2 cups basmati rice, washed several
   times

1 1/4 tsp salt
2 handfuls of peas, fresh or frozen
3 cups water

1 Heat the oil in a saucepan for 1 minute. Add the cumin seeds and wait for about 1–2 minutes until they start popping.

2 Add the onion and fry (sauté) gently over a medium heat for 3 minutes until it turns golden brown.

3 Add the rice and salt and stir well to coat all the grains with the cumin and onion mixture.

4 Mix in the peas and stir well.

5 Add the water, bring to the boil, then reduce the heat and simmer for 10–12 minutes.

6 Remove from the heat, stir and stand for 5 minutes to finish cooking by itself before serving.

Photograph opposite:
Indian Cheese-flavoured Rice (page 100) with Peas and Rice (page 97) and Fresh Punjabi Chapattis (page 104).

Khooshboo Elachi Chawal

AROMATIC CARDAMOM RICE

Delicate grains of basmati rice flavoured with aromatic cardamom pods and garam masala, this is delicious with just about any meat, fish or vegetable curry. Using green cardamom pods rather than brown will ensure that their flavour doesn't overwhelm the attractive fragrance of this dish.

serves 4–6 | preparation 5 minutes | cooking 15 minutes

1¹/₂ cups basmati rice, washed several times
3 cups water
1¹/₄ tsp garam masala

1¹/₄ tsp salt
1¹/₂ tsp butter
3–4 green cardamom pods, crushed
a large handful of peas, fresh or frozen

1 Place all the ingredients in a saucepan.

2 Bring to boil for 3 minutes, then stir, reduce the heat and simmer for about 10–12 minutes until the water has evaporated.

3 Remove from the heat and stand for 5 minutes to finish cooking by itself before serving.

Masala Chawal

SPICED RICE

This is Win sister's alternative to Khooshboo Elachi Chawal (see above), another rice dish to enjoy with any meat, fish or vegetable curry. It's spiced up with cloves and cumin seeds for a more robust flavour. You can remove the cardamom pods and cloves before serving if you prefer.

serves 4–6 | preparation 5 minutes | cooking 15 minutes

1¹/₂ cups basmati rice, washed several times
3 cups water
1¹/₄ tsp garam masala
1¹/₄ tsp salt

1¹/₂ tsp butter
3–4 green cardamom pods, crushed
4 whole cloves
1¹/₂ tsp cumin seeds
a handful of peas, fresh or frozen

1 Place all the ingredients in a saucepan.

2 Bring to boil for 3 minutes, then stir, reduce the heat and simmer for about 10–12 minutes until the water has evaporated.

3 Remove from the heat, stir again and stand for 5 minutes to finish cooking by itself before serving.

SERVING SUGGESTIONS AND TIPS

- You could add a few drops of yellow, orange or red food colouring to portions of the rice to create coloured – or even multi-coloured – rice for a special occasion.

Desi Fried Chawal

INDIAN FRIED RICE

This makes a dish of light and fluffy rice with onions and cumin seeds to give it an exotic taste. You can enjoy it with any meat, fish or vegetable curry – just about any Indian dish, in fact. Its unassuming flavour complements so many dishes it makes it really versatile.

serves 4–6 | preparation 5 minutes | cooking 20 minutes

2 tbsp olive oil
1¹/₂ tsp cumin seeds
1 large onion, finely sliced
1¹/₂ cups basmati rice, washed several
   times

1¹/₄ tsp salt
3 cups water

1 Heat the oil in a saucepan for 1 minute. Add the cumin seeds and wait for about 1–2 minutes until they start popping.

2 Add the onion and fry (sauté) gently over a medium heat for 3 minutes until it turns golden brown.

3 Add the rice and salt and stir well to coat all the grains with the cumin and onion mixture.

4 Add the water, bring to the boil, then reduce the heat and simmer for 14 minutes.

5 Remove from the heat, stir and stand for 5 minutes to finish cooking by itself before serving.

Paneer Pilau

INDIAN CHEESE-FLAVOURED RICE

Nutritious and appetising cubes of paneer cooked with fragrant grains of basmati rice, the queen of all rices, makes this a very statisfying meal in itself or an accompaniment to any curries. The paneer has a meat-like texture, fused with gorgeous sweet-smelling and flavoursome spices.

serves 4 | preparation 5 minutes | cooking 15 minutes

a few saffron strands (optional)
3 tbsp olive oil
1 large handful of fried paneer cubes
  (see page 16)
1¼ tsp salt
4 whole cloves
¼ tsp freshly ground black pepper
1½ tsp cumin seeds

2 bay leaves
3 brown cardamom pods
1 or 2 cinnamon sticks
1½ cups basmati rice, washed several
  times
3 cups water
a few drops of lemon juice

1 If using, soak the saffron strands in 1 tbsp of water and set aside.

2 Heat the oil in a medium saucepan. Add the paneer, the salt and all the spices and fry (sauté) for 5 minutes.

3 Add the rice and stir to coat all the grains in the spice mixture.

4 Discard the saffron threads, if using, and add the soaking liquid to the pan with the water and lemon juice. Bring to the boil, then reduce the heat and simmer for 10–12 minutes, stirring occasionally, until the rice is almost cooked.

5 Remove from the heat and leave to stand for a few minutes to finish cooking by itself before serving.

SERVING SUGGESTIONS AND TIPS

• Serve with any meat, fish or vegetable curry.

• As a variation, add mixed vegetables, cut into bite-sized pieces, or a diced chicken breast at step 2.

Rotis

BREADS

Breads are often an integral part of an Indian meal and even the simplest are very satisfying. Hot chappatis straight from the griddle (thava) are very typical, certainly in our households, and accompany most vegetable and meat curries. Richer breads, such as naans and bhaturey, are served on grand occasions — weddings, social gatherings, birthdays and parties for instance.

Breads are also versatile in that they can be enjoyed simply on their own or can be turned into a complete dish by stuffing them with dhal, fried onions or mashed potatoes and lightly fried to provide a hearty breakfast or brunch. Just add butter, pickles and yoghurt and enjoy!

Krishna Ji's Tandoori Roti

KRISHNA JI'S TANDOORI CHAPATTIS

Tandoori roti is traditionally cooked in a tandoor, but Babita's inventive mum uses her own alternatives – a flat-surfaced frying pan and the grill! These are most frequently made plain and served with a melting knob of butter on top – simply delicious with any meat or vegetable curry.

makes 6 | preparation 15 minutes | resting 15–20 minutes | cooking 5 minutes each

1¹/₂ **cups plain (all-purpose) flour, plus extra for dusting**

¹/₂ **cup cold water, plus extra for sprinkling butter, for spreading**

1 Place the flour and water in a deep bowl. Lightly flour your 'mixing' hand and, holding the bowl with the other hand, mix the flour and water to a sticky dough. Knead for 2 minutes to form a smooth dough, then cover and leave to rest for 15–20 minutes.

2 Dust a work surface lightly with flour and dust both hands. Divide the dough into six equal portions. Holding one portion in the palm of one hand, knead it three or four times with the other (this allows lots of air to get into the roti and encourages it to rise).

3 Roll the dough into a ball in the palm of both hands (you may need to flour your hands again).

4 Place the ball on a floured surface and flatten it to a round about 7.5 cm/3 in in diameter. Using a rolling pin, roll it out until it is roughly the size of a side plate (about 20 cm/8 in). Repeat with the other five portions.

5 Heat a frying pan (skillet) until it is very hot. Lower it to medium heat, then pick up one roti and slap it on to the centre of the pan.

6 Cook for 3–4 minutes until lightly browned with darker spots, then remove the roti and sprinkle cold water on the uncooked side.

7 Throw the roti, uncooked side up, under a preheated grill (broiler). The roti should balloon up with the fierce heat (this provides the tandoor effect). Cook until golden brown and darker spots are appearing. If necessary, turn the roti over again and cook this side a little more.

8 Remove from the pan and wrap in foil or a clean tea towel (dish cloth) to keep warm while cooking the remaining rotis. Top with a knob of butter and serve.

Dahi te Dudh Wale Sada Naan

YOGHURT AND MILK PLAIN NAANS

Soft, light and scrumptious and best eaten hot, these lush-tasting naan breads are made with creamy natural yoghurt and milk and are then lightly grilled or baked. Naan bread is traditionally made in a 'tandoor', an Indian clay oven. They are great as part of an Indian menu for special dinner parties or just with dips.

makes 6 | preparation 15 minutes | resting 30 minutes | cooking 15 minutes

2³/₄ cups self-raising (self-rising flour), plus extra for rolling
³/₄ tsp salt
2¹/₂ tbsp cumin or black onion seeds
¹/₂ tsp baking powder

3 tsp/1 sachet of fast-acting dried yeast
1 cup lukewarm milk
3 tbsp melted butter of ghee, plus extra for brushing
2 tbsp plain yoghurt

1 Mix together the flour, salt, 1¹/₂ tsp of the cumin seeds or black onion seeds, the baking powder and yeast in a large bowl. Add the milk and mix lightly by hand or with a wooden spoon.

2 Add the melted butter or ghee and yoghurt and combine to make a soft dough. Cover with a tea towel (dish cloth) and leave to rest for 30 minutes.

3 Knead the dough for 2–4 minutes until smooth, then divide equally into six portions. Using lightly floured hands, roll each portion into a ball and knead lightly with the palm of your hand. Roll and shape each ball on a lightly floured surface into a round or pear shape, no less than 5mm/¹/₄ in thick.

4 Brush with melted butter or ghee and cook under a preheated grill (broiler) for 4 minutes on each side, or bake in a preheated oven at 190°C/375°F/gas mark 5/ fan oven 170°C for 8–10 minutes until lightly browned on each side. Sprinkle with the remaining cumin or black onion seeds.

SERVING SUGGESTION AND TIPS

- Serve with any curry, or use as wraps with starters, or cut up for dips.

- You can replace the yoghurt with double (heavy) cream for extra creamy naans.

- For garlic and coriander (cilantro) naans, substitute crushed garlic or garlic paste and chopped coriander for the cumin seeds and cook as above.

- Use wholemeal flour for a healthier version – or you could use half wholemeal dough and half plain dough, as above, roughly combined to create marbled naans.

Tazhee Punjabi Roti

FRESH PUNJABI CHAPATTIS

There's nothing to beat the taste of a fresh, hot roti straight from a heated thava. Making them is a skill that takes time and practice to master, one that is usually learned by daughters at their mother's side from an early age. Our mums are experts and so fast they can make ten to fifteen in 20 minutes!

makes 6–8 | preparation 15 minutes | resting 15–20 minutes | cooking 5 minutes each

1½ cups wholewheat flour, plus extra for dusting

½ cup cold water

1 Place the flour in a deep bowl and add the water. Lightly flour your 'mixing' hand and, holding the bowl with the other hand, thoroughly mix together the flour and water to form a sticky dough.

2 Knead for 2 minutes to form a smooth dough, then cover and leave to rest for 15–20 minutes.

3 Dust a work surface lightly with flour and dust both hands. Tear off a piece of dough about the size of a clementine. Holding it in the palm of one hand, knead it three or four times with the other (this allows lots of air to get into the roti and encourages it to rise).

4 Roll the dough into a ball in the palm of both hands (you may need to flour your hands again).

5 Place the ball on a floured surface and flatten it to a round about 7.5 cm/3 in in diameter. Using a rolling pin, roll it out until it is roughly the size of a side plate (about 20 cm/8 in). Repeat the tearing off, kneading and rolling until all the dough is used up.

6 Heat a frying pan (skillet) until it is very hot. Lower it to a medium heat, then pick up one roti and slap it on to the centre of the pan.

7 Cook for 30–60 seconds until bubbles begin to appear on the surface. Flip the roti over using tongs and cook the other side for about 1 minute. Turn the roti again and, using a scrunched-up tea towel (dish cloth), press down all the way round the roti for about 1 minute. The roti should begin to rise.

8 Flip the roti and repeat the pressing down on the other side for about 1 minute. Repeat the flipping and pressing until the roti is cooked to lightly brown on both sides.

9 Remove from the pan and wrap in foil or a clean tea towel to keep warm while cooking the remaining rotis.

SERVING SUGGESTIONS AND TIPS

- Serve with any savoury curry.
- Rotis can be made an hour beforehand and reheated before serving the meal (microwave on Full for 30 seconds).
- For lighter rotis, use plain (all-purpose) flour.
- It is preferable to use a flat-surfaced frying pan rather than a grooved one.

Ghee Wala Sada Paratha

BUTTERED PLAIN CRISPY FLAT BREADS

A classic Punjabi bread typically served as a hearty weekend breakfast for the whole family, this certainly sets you up for the rest of the day! Parathas are softer than roti, and these ones just ooze with luscious oil or melted butter. They can also be stuffed to make a more substantial breakfast or snack (see below).

makes 6–8 | preparation 15 minutes | resting 20 minutes | cooking 5 minutes each

2 cups wholewheat flour, plus extra for
    dusting
$^1/_2$ cup water

2 tbsp butter or olive oil
salt and garam masala, for sprinkling
butter, for spreading

1 Place the flour in a deep bowl and add the water. Lightly flour your 'mixing' hand and, holding the bowl with the other hand, thoroughly mix together the flour and water to form a sticky dough.

2 Knead for 2–4 minutes to form a smooth dough, then cover and leave to rest for 15–20 minutes.

3 Dust a work surface lightly with flour and dust both hands. Tear off a piece of dough about the size of a satsuma and roll it into a ball in the palm of your hands. Flatten the ball between your hands, then dip it into the dusting flour and, using a rolling pin, roll it out to a round about the size of a saucer (15 cm/6 in).

4 Thinly spread the centre with the butter or olive oil and add a sprinkling of salt and garam masala. Fold the top third of the round down to the middle and press flat. Fold the bottom third up to the middle, then fold both sides into the middle to form a 15–20 cm/6–8 in square. Repeat the tearing off, rolling, spreading, sprinkling and folding until all the dough is used up.

5 Heat a flat-surfaced frying pan (skillet) until it is very hot. Lower it to a medium heat, then pick up one paratha and slap it on to the centre of the pan.

6 Cook for 1–2 minutes until bubbles begin to appear on the surface. Flip the paratha over using tongs and cook the other side for a further 1–2 minutes.

7 Smear more butter or olive oil all over the paratha and cook for 5 seconds until golden brown. Flip over again and repeat until the paratha is cooked and browned and darker spots have appeared on both sides.

8 Remove from the pan and wrap in foil or a clean tea towel (dish cloth) to keep warm while cooking the remaining parathas.

9 Eat spread with butter.

SERVING SUGGESTIONS AND TIPS

- Eat with pickles of your choice and plain yoghurt as accompaniments.
- Serve with curries instead of chapattis.

Pooris

DEEP-FRIED BREAD ROUNDS

Delicious, melt-in-the-mouth bread rounds, pooris use only the simplest of ingredients and take almost no time to prepare and cook, making them an ideal acompaniment to everyday meals. Once fried, they puff up to make a delightfully light accompaniment to any spicy meat, fish or vegetable curry.

makes 8–10 | preparation 10 minutes | resting 20 minutes | cooking 2–4 minutes each

1 cup wholewheat flour
2 cups plain (all-purpose) flour, plus extra
  for dusting

1 tbsp olive oil
2¹/₂ cups water
oil for deep-frying

1 Mix together the flours and oil.

2 Add the water and knead the dough. Leave to rest for 20 minutes.

3 Using lightly floured hands, tear off a piece of dough about the size of a walnut. Using a rolling pin, roll it out to a round about the size of a saucer (15 cm/6 in).

4 Heat the oil until hot, carefully drop in one round and fry (sauté) until golden brown and puffed up. Remove, drain on a kitchen paper (paper towel) and keep warm while making the remaining pooris.

SERVING SUGGESTIONS AND TIPS

- These pooris can be made beforehand and reheated in the oven or microwave.
- Although traditionally served plain with wet curries, they can also be spiced up. Just add 1 tsp of garam masala, 1 tsp cumin seeds and ¹/₂ tsp of hot chilli powder to the flour and mix to combine before adding the oil.

Ghee te Aloo Deh Paratha

BUTTERED POTATO-STUFFED CRISPY FLAT BREADS

Punjabis are renowned for this dish – freshly cooked, crispy flat breads stuffed with mashed potato and spread with golden, melted butter. An absolutely heavenly dish and one that is a real treat for a weekend breakfast; just the smell wafting from the hot griddle is enough to make your taste buds water.

makes 4–6 | preparation 15 minutes | resting 20 minutes | cooking 5 minutes each

2 cups plain (all-purpose) or wholewheat flour, plus extra for dusting
1 cup water
1 large baking potato
1 small onion, finely chopped (optional)

2 green finger chillies, finely chopped
1 tsp salt
1 tbsp garam masala
1 tbsp butter, plus extra for spreading

1 Place the flour in a deep bowl and add the water. Lightly flour your 'mixing' hand and, holding the bowl with the other hand, thoroughly mix together the flour and water to form a sticky dough.

2 Knead for 2–4 minutes to form a smooth dough, then cover and leave to rest for 15–20 minutes.

3 Meanwhile, microwave the potato on High for 8 minutes. Allow to cool slightly, then mash in a large bowl with a potato masher. Add the onion, if using, chillies, salt, garam masala and butter and mix roughly.

4 Dust a work surface lightly with flour and dust both hands. Tear off a piece of dough about the size of a satsuma and roll it into a ball in the palm of your hands. Flatten the ball between your hands, then dip it into the dusting flour and, using a rolling pin, roll it out to a round about the size of a side plate (20 cm/ 8 in). Repeat with a second satsuma-sized piece of dough.

5 Take 3–4 tbsp of the potato filling and spread it evenly on to one dough round, leaving a 5 cm/¹/₂ in gap all round. Gently pick up the second round and place it on the first. Seal the filling into the paratha by pressing lightly with your fingers. Repeat the tearing off, rolling, filling and pairing until all the dough is used up.

6 Heat a frying pan (skillet) until it is very hot. Lower it to a medium heat, then pick up one paired paratha (use a spatula if necessary) and slap it on to the centre of the pan.

7 Cook for 1-2 minutes until bubbles begin to appear on the surface. Flip the paratha over using tongs and cook the other side for 1–2 minutes.

8 Spread butter all over the paratha and cook for 5 seconds until golden brown. Turn the paratha over, spread the other side with butter and cook for a further 5 seconds. Flip over again and repeat until the paratha is cooked and browned and darker spots have appeared on both sides.

9 Remove from the pan and wrap in foil or a clean tea towel (dish cloth) to keep warm while cooking the remaining parathas. Eat topped with a knob of melting butter.

SERVING SUGGESTIONS AND TIPS

- Eat simply with pickles of your choice and plain yoghurt as accompaniments.
- These can be stuffed with other fillings, such as grated white Indian radish (muli) or raw grated cauliflower.
- It is preferable to use a flat-surfaced frying pan rather than a grooved one.

Sadi Maki Ki Roti

PLAIN CORNMEAL FLAT BREADS

*Sweet-tasting, hot cornmeal breads often served with saag (mixed curried greens) as
a main meal. The simplicity and taste of these well-known Punjabi breads create a
cracking complement to greens, as well as a striking, contrasting yellow colour.
Spread with melting butter before eating – scrumptious!*

makes 4 | preparation 15 minutes | cooking 5 minutes each

³/₄ **cup fine yellow cornmeal**
³/₄ **cup medium or coarse yellow cornmeal**

1 cup slightly cooled boiled water
butter, for spreading

1 Mix together the two cornmeals in a bowl. Add the water and mix with a spatula
until a firm dough has formed.

2 Lightly flour your hands and tear the dough into four equal pieces. Roll one piece
into a ball in the palm of your hands until it is smooth and no cracks are seen.

3 Split open a plastic food bag and place the ball on it. Gently press the ball with
one hand and begin rotating and patting it until the dough is a round the size of
a side plate (about 20 cm/8 in). Repeat the tearing off, rolling and pressing with
the remaining pieces of dough.

4 Heat a non-stick frying pan (skillet) until it is very hot. Gently place one dough
round on the pan (use a spatula if necessary) and cook for about 2–3 minutes.

5 Turn the roti over with a spatula and cook the other side for 2–3 minutes until
crisped, golden-brown and darker spots have appeared on both sides. Press
down with the spatula to ensure the roti is cooked through.

6 Remove from the pan and wrap in foil or a clean tea towel (dish cloth) to keep
warm while cooking the remaining rotis.

7 Spread one side with butter and serve.

SERVING SUGGESTIONS AND TIPS

- Serve traditionally with delicious Satpal's Sada Bahar Saag (see page 59).
- It is preferable to use a flat-surfaced frying pan rather than a grooved one.
- Try this for another another delicious Punjabi breakfast: add a handful of fenugreek
leaves to the dough to make Methi Ki Roti and cook in a frying pan as above. Serve
with butter, a choice of pickles and plain yoghurt as accompaniments.

Dahi Wale Bhaturey

YOGHURT AND MILK DEEP-FRIED BREADS

*Delicious, melt-in-your-mouth, rich, fluffy fried bread rounds, softened with light,
creamy yoghurt, this variation of traditional bhaturey has added potato to give
them a softer and lighter texture. They are popular as a treat and on grand
occasions, particularly weddings, and are usually served with wet curries.*

makes about 16 | **preparation 10 minutes** | **resting 20 minutes** | **cooking 2–4 minutes each**

1 large baking potato
2 tbsp vegetable or olive oil
2 cups self-raising (self-rising) flour, plus
  extra for dusting

1/4 tsp salt
3 tbsp plain yoghurt
1 cup lukewarm milk
2 1/2 cups oil for deep-frying

1 Microwave the potato on High for 8 minutes. Allow to cool, then scoop out the
  inside and place in a bowl. Add the oil and mash thoroughly.

2 Mix in the flour, salt and yoghurt.

3 Add the milk a little at a time, mixing with lightly floured hands between each
  addition to form a dough.

4 Knead the dough until smooth, then cover with a tea towel (dish cloth) and leave
  to rest for 20 minutes.

5 Tear off a piece of dough about the size of a walnut. Place it on a lightly floured
  work surface and, using a rolling pin, roll it out to a round about the size of a
  saucer (15 cm/6 in). Repeat the tearing off and rolling until all the dough is used
  up.

6 Heat the oil for deep-frying in a frying pan (skillet) and fry (sauté) the bhatureys
  one at a time until golden brown and puffed up.

7 Remove from the pan and wrap in foil or a clean tea towel (dish cloth) to keep
  warm while cooking the remaining bhatureys.

SERVING SUGGESTIONS AND TIPS

- These are most popular served with Tari Wale Aloo Chole (see page 45), but they
  are a great accompaniment to other curries too.

- The potato can be omitted for a more traditional recipe.

Mithi Ki Cheej

SOMETHING SWEET

In Northern India the desserts are made from rich, wholesome ingredients such as fruit, milk and clarified butter. These sweet luxuries are given to people on auspicious occasions – such as the festival of Diwali – and to wedding guests, and families and friends bring them to your house in much the same way as guests here might bring a bottle of wine.

The desserts range from the traditional Pista Dudh Ki Barfi (Pistachio Milk Fudge, see page 123) and Khooshboo Dar Kheer (Aromatic Rice Pudding, see page 119) to improvised 'Hinglish' desserts such as Am te Anar Cheesecake (Mango and Pomegranate Cheesecake, see page 117).

Elachi, Pista te Badam Ki Kulfi

CARDAMOM, PISTACHIO AND ALMOND ICE-CREAM

A dessert fit for a king, this recipe gives a much quicker way to make Indian ice-cream than the traditional method, which involves boiling milk down to thick solids. Kulfi uses natural, wholesome, creamy ingredients to create a rich and tempting dessert that is a real luxury to eat.

serves 6–8 | preparation 10 minutes | freezing 2–2¹/₂ hours

¹/₂ cup double (heavy) cream
1¹/₄ cups evaporated milk
¹/₂ tsp ground cardamom (see below)
3 tbsp caster (superfine) sugar

3 tbsp unsalted pistachio nuts, chopped
a few drops of almond essence (extract)
1¹/₂ tbsp flaked (slivered) almonds,
  to decorate

1 Whisk the cream in a large bowl until stiff peaks form. Add the evaporated milk, ground cardamom, sugar, half the pistachios and the almond essence and whisk for 1–2 minutes. Transfer to a container suitable for freezing.

2 Freeze for about 1 hour, then remove and whisk with a fork to break up any ice crystals.

3 Return to the freezer and freeze for a further 1–1¹/₂ hours.

4 Decorate with the flaked almonds and reserved pistachios and serve. Alternatively, freeze in individual ice cream or kulfi moulds and keep in the freezer for up to 3 months.

SERVING SUGGESTIONS AND TIPS

- Substitute the pulp of a fresh mango or 1 cup of canned mango pulp for the almonds and pistachios to make an easy mango kulfi.

- Substitute vanilla essence for the pistachios, almonds and almond essence to make vanilla kulfi.

- If you keep cardamom pods rather than ground cardamom, you will need to extract and crush about 20 seeds (the contents of 4–5 pods) to give you ¹/₂ teaspoonful. The advantage of using pods is that cardamom is one of the spices that loses its essential oil once crushed.

Sanjay's Am Ki Kulfi

SANJAY'S MANGO ICE-CREAM

This ice-cream is made the traditional Indian way by Babita's husband, Sanjay. It's quite time-consuming but the result is well worth the effort and the wait. Indian ice-cream is richer, creamier and sweeter in taste than Western ice-cream so you might want to keep the portions quite small.

serves 6–8 | preparation 40 minutes | freezing 5 hours

3 or 4 fresh ripe mangos
²/₃ cup full-fat milk
1 tbsp ground rice
250 ml/8 fl oz/small can of evaporated milk
1 tsp cardamom seeds (from about 10 whole green pods)

2 cups double (heavy) cream
1 tbsp sugar
1 tbsp rose water or vanilla essence (extract)
Chopped pistachio nuts, to decorate (optional)

1 Slice the mangos, remove and discard the stone (pit) and scoop out the flesh. Whiz the flesh in a blender for 1 minute to purée.

2 Place the ground rice in a saucepan. Heat the full-fat milk until lukewarm, then gradually add to the rice, stirring constantly to avoid lumps.

3 Heat the evaporated milk in a separate saucepan until it boils. Add the cardamon seeds and remove from the heat.

4 Gradually add the evaporated milk to the ground rice mixture, stirring constantly, then stir in the cream, sugar and mango purée. Cook the mixture on a medium heat for 12–15 minutes, stirring constantly.

5 Remove from the heat, allow to cool for a couple of minutes, then add the rose water or vanilla. Stir and mix well.

6 Allow the mixture to cool completely, stirring occasionally to prevent a skin forming on the surface.

7 When completely cooled, transfer the mixture to kulfi containers, plastic ice-cream pots or other freezer containers. Decorate with the pistachio nuts, if using. Freeze for at least 5 hours, then transfer to the fridge for an hour to soften before serving.

SERVING SUGGESTIONS AND TIPS

- You could use a 450 g/1 lb/large can of mango instead of fresh.

Tundhi Am Di Malai

CHILLED MANGO CREAMED BLANCMANGE

A milky mango cream dessert created by Win for people who love a refreshing dessert but prefer something not as cold as ice-cream. If you have gelatine powder in a pot, 2 teaspoonfuls is the equivalent of 1 sachet, or you can use 6 leaves of gelatine. Vege-gel is a vegetarian setting agent containing carrageen.

serves 4 | preparation 5 minutes | chilling 40 minutes | cooking 15 minutes

1½ cups semi-skimmed milk
flesh of 1 large, ripe mango
  or 1 cup canned pulp
2 tbsp demerera, granulated or caster
  (superfine) sugar

2 tbsp vege-gel or 1 sachet of gelatine
sweetened desiccated (shredded)
  coconut or flaked (slivered) almonds,
  to decorate

1 Pour the milk into a saucepan. Add the mango, sugar and vege-gel or gelatine, stirring well to avoid lumps. Bring to the boil, stirring frequently.

2 When thickened, remove from the heat and allow to cool slightly.

3 Pour into ramekins (custard cups) or a large dish and chill for 40 minutes.

4 Serve decorated with desiccated coconut or flaked almonds.

SERVING SUGGESTIONS AND TIPS

- This is delicious served with a drizzle of cream or a scoop of vanilla ice-cream.
- Add 4 or 5 whole cloves to the milk for a spicier taste. Remember to remove them before chilling.
- Substitute a few tablespoons of coconut milk and grated fresh or sweetened desiccated coconut for the mango pulp and add a little extra sugar to make a delicious coconut cream dessert. Decorate with chopped fruit.

Desi Phal te Dahi

INDIAN FRESH FRUITS WITH YOGHURT

A healthy way to complete your meal, this is a combination of fresh, exotic Indian fruits topped with lashings of smooth, creamy crème fraîche and Greek yoghurt. You can experiment with your favourite combinations of fruits according to the season and what is available.

serves 6–8 | preparation 10 minutes

3 medium mangos
18 fresh lychees
1 medium honeydew melon

1 large pomegranate
5 tbsp half-fat crème fraîche
5 tbsp Greek yoghurt

1 Halve the mangos and remove the stone (pit). Using a sharp knife, mark the flesh into cubes, then turn inside-out to get a 'hedgehog' effect. Place each half in a separate serving dish.

2 Peel the lychees and rinse through with cold water. Divide equally between the dishes.

3 Halve the melon and remove the seeds. Cut into slices, then use a sharp knife to cut cubes of flesh away from the skin. Divide equally between the dishes.

4 Cut the pomegranate into wedges and remove the seeds from the pith. Divide the seeds between the dishes.

5 Mix together the crème fraîche and yoghurt until smooth. Dollop on top of the fruit and serve.

Khooshboo Dar Kheer

AROMATIC RICE PUDDING

Satisfying, creamy rice pudding cooked with nutty almonds and sweet-smelling cardamom seeds, finished off with a few drops of delicately scented rose water. This is a truly aromatic dessert! If you use whole cardamom pods, don't forget to remove them before serving, or they can be left at the side of your plate.

serves 4–6 | preparation 10 minutes | cooking 20 minutes

½ cup pudding rice, thoroughly washed and rinsed

1 cup water

2½ cups full-fat milk

3 tbsp flaked (slivered) almonds

crushed seeds from 4 whole green cardamom pods

2–3 tbsp granulated or caster (superfine) sugar

5–8 drops of rose water

1 Place the rice in a heavy-based saucepan, add the water and bring to the boil over a medium heat.

2 Stir in the milk. Reduce the heat and cook for 12–15 minutes, stirring constantly so the rice does not stick to the bottom of the pan.

3 Add the almonds and crushed cardamom seeds and cook for a further 5 minutes.

4 Add the sugar and stir. Cook for a further 2 minutes.

5 Remove from the heat, add the rose water and stir.

6 Serve hot or cold.

SERVING SUGGESTIONS AND TIPS

- Add a strand of saffron to the rice with the water to add colour to the pudding.

Am te Anar Cheesecake

MANGO AND POMEGRANATE CHEESECAKE

Complete indulgence, this desert is cooling, refreshing and full of delight! The combination of crème fraîche, soft cheese and thick Greek yoghurt makes it ultra-creamy. It only takes a few minutes to prepare, but you do need to allow the necessary time for it to set.

serves 4–6 | preparation 15 minutes | setting 1 hour

250 g/9 oz digestive biscuits (graham crackers)
8 tbsp butter
150 ml/¼ pt/small pot of half-fat crème fraîche
5 tbsp half-fat soft cheese

5 tbsp Greek yoghurt
1 egg white, whipped into stiff peaks, or ½ sachet of vege-gel or gelatine (optional)
1 large ripe mango
a large handful of pomegranate seeds

1 Place the biscuits in a plastic bag, leaving at least 5 cm/2 in of space at the top (if your bag isn't big enough, just crush the biscuits in more than one batch).

2 Remove the excess air from the bag and seal the end (we usually tie a knot). Using the flat end of a rolling pin, crush and grind the biscuits to crumbs. Pour into a small shallow serving dish.

3 Melt the butter in a small pan over a medium heat (or melt briefly in the microwave) and add to the biscuit crumbs. Stir in until the biscuits are covered with the butter. Pat the biscuit and butter mixture with the back of a large serving spoon to get a smooth base. Cover with clingfilm (plastic wrap) and chill for at least 1 hour until set.

4 Using a fork, mix together the crème fraîche, cheese and yoghurt in a mixing bowl. Fold in the egg white or vege-gel, if using (this will give a stiff cream cheese). Cover with clingfilm and chill for at least 45 minutes until set.

5 When the biscuit base has set, scoop up the cheese mixture and place it on top of the biscuit base. Working from the middle outwards, spread it evenly over the base.

6 Peel the mango and cut the flesh into slices. Use to decorate the top of the cheesecake and finish with a sprinkling of pomegranate seeds.

7 Cover loosely with clingfilm and chill until ready to serve.

SERVING SUGGESTIONS AND TIPS

- If it seems difficult to spread the topping over the biscuit base, then the base should be returned to the fridge to set for longer.

Rasmalai

JUICY PANEER BALLS

A fine dessert enjoyed on many special occasions – luscious, sweet milk balls (malai) served in a creamy syrup fragranced with cardamom and decorated with pistachios (ras). Traditionally made from paneer and reduced sweetened milk, this recipe is much quicker, especially if you use bought paneer. It's just as delicious with tofu.

makes 16 | preparation 20 minutes | cooking 10 minutes

For the malai
250 g/9 oz bought or home-made paneer
3 tbsp semolina (cream of wheat)
For the ras
5 cups water
2¹/₂ cups granulated sugar

A few drops of rose water (optional)
300 ml/¹/₂ pint/medium pot of single (light) cream
crushed seeds from 4 whole green cardamom pods
2 tsp crushed pistachio nuts

1 If making the paneer, follow steps 1–3 of the recipe on page 16. Using a tea towel (dish cloth) or muslin, squeeze out the excess water. If using bought paneer, whiz the paneer in a blender for 1 minute and transfer to a mixing bowl.

2 Add the semolina to the paneer and mix by hand. Take a walnut-size piece and roll and press it firmly to make a slightly flattened ball. Repeat with the remaining mixture.

3 Transfer the rounds to a microwaveable plate and microwave on Medium for 3 minutes. Set aside.

4 To make the ras, bring the water and sugar to the boil in a large saucepan. Add the rose water, if using. Reduce the heat and carefully add the paneer balls. Cook for 10 minutes to absorb the sweet syrup.

5 Remove the paneer balls. Allow to cool, then chill for 1 hour.

6 Just before serving, mix together the cream, crushed cardamom and crushed pistachios and serve with the paneer balls.

Kadoo Kas Gajrella Halwa

GRATED CARROT DESSERT

Kadoo Kas Gajrella Halwa is a lovely, brightly coloured, thick and wholesome dessert made from grated carrots and milk, subtly fragranced with cardamom, almonds and sultanas. A heavenly and creamy combination, it is easy to make and takes very little time for stunning, authentic results.

serves 4–6 | preparation 10 minutes | cooking 40 minutes

3³/₄ cups milk
6 carrots, grated
crushed seeds from 6–8 whole green
  cardamom pods
2–3 tbsp unsalted (sweet) butter or ghee

5 tbsp granulated or caster (superfine)
  sugar
2 tbsp sultanas (golden raisins)
4 tbsp flaked (slivered) almonds

1 Bring the milk to the boil in a heavy-based saucepan. Add the carrots and crushed cardamom seeds.

2 Lower the heat and cook for 30–40 minutes until all the liquid is absorbed.

3 Add the butter or ghee, sugar, sultanas and 3 tbsp of the flaked almonds. Cook for a further 5 minutes until the texture is glazed and shiny.

4 Serve hot or cold, decorated with the reserved flaked almonds.

Photograph opposite:
Lemon Pickle (page 140), Onion, Tomato and Chilli
Relish (page 135), Yoghurt and Milk Deep-fried Breads
(page 111) and Plain Cornmeal Flatbreads (page 110).

Sooji Ka Halwa

SEMOLINA DESSERT

Sweetened semolina, cooked in butter, with sweet sultanas, rich almonds and subtly aromatic cardamon pods, this makes a rich, gooey and thick dessert. It is served to the whole congregation at gurdwaras – Sikh temples – and other temples and is called prashad, meaning 'sacred pudding' as it is blessed beforehand.

serves 4–6 | preparation 10 minutes | cooking 40 minutes

2¹/₂ cups water
1¹/₄ cups sugar
1¹/₄ cups unsalted (sweet) butter or ghee
1¹/₄ cups semolina (cream of wheat)

¹/₄ cup sultanas (golden raisins)
¹/₄ cup flaked (slivered) almonds
crushed seeds from 4–5 whole green cardamom pods

1 Place the water and sugar in a heavy-based saucepan. Bring to the boil and stir constantly until the sugar has dissolved. Remove from the heat.

2 In another saucepan, melt the butter or ghee on a very low heat. Add the semolina and cook, stirring constantly, until golden brown and the butter bubbles to the top.

3 Lower the heat and add the syrup from other pan, stirring constantly until the halwa becomes a thick mixture.

4 Remove from the heat and add the sultanas, half the flaked almonds and the crushed cardamom seeds.

5 Decorate with the remaining flaked almonds and serve.

Photograph opposite:
Grated Carrot Dessert (page 120)
with Pistachio Milk Fudge (page 123).

Rasila Gulab Jaman

JUICY SEMOLINA BALLS

*Soft semolina balls drenched in a gorgeous, sweet syrup. They can be served cold
but are absolutely scrumptious while still warm and are a real treat for guests
whatever the occasion. A classic Punjabi dessert and one that is very well liked by
all. The Punjabi name for semolina is sooji.*

makes 16 | preparation 45 minutes | cooking 15 minutes

For the gulab jaman
¹/₂ cup milk
¹/₄ cup semolina (cream of wheat)
¹/₄ cup self-raising (self-rising) flour
¹/₂ tsp baking powder
¹/₄ tsp bicarbonate of soda (baking soda)
1³/₄ cups full-fat dried milk powder (dry milk)
crushed seeds from 4–5 whole green
    cardamom pods (optional)

1¹/₂ tbsp melted unsalted (sweet) butter,
    plus extra for greasing
2¹/₂ cups vegetable oil
1 tsp desiccated (shredded) coconut, to
    decorate
For the syrup
1¹/₂ cups granulated or soft brown sugar
2 cups water

1 To make the gulab jamans, heat half the milk to lukewarm, add the semolina and
leave to soak for 20 minutes.

2 Mix the flour, baking powder, bicarbonate of soda, milk powder, cardamom, if
using, and butter into the semolina mixture with a spatula to make a soft dough.
Mix in the remaining milk a little at a time, then leave to set for 15 minutes.

3 With lightly greased hands, shape walnut-sized pieces of the dough into balls.

4 Heat the oil until hot in a frying pan (skillet) or wok, lower the heat and fry
(sauté) the gulab jamans a few at a time, turning frequently and pressing down to
ensure they are cooked through, until golden brown. Remove from the oil and
place on kitchen paper (paper towels) to drain. Set aside.

5 To make the syrup, place the sugar and water in a saucepan and bring to the boil.
Reduce the heat and stir constantly until the sugar has dissolved. Remove from
the heat. Add the gulab jamans to the syrup, turning them to soak them
completely. Decorate with the coconut and serve.

SERVING SUGGESTIONS AND TIPS

• If the syrup begins to crystallise, gently microwave.

Pista Dudh Ki Barfi

PISTACHIO MILK FUDGE

Delicious, wholesome and extremely popular, these fudgy pieces are made from milk, sugar and cream. They are great with a cup of hot Masala Chai (see page 130) in the afternoon. Why not experiment by adding a few drops of red or green food colouring to create your own colourful barfi?

makes 15–20 | preparation 10 minutes | cooking 5 minutes | setting 1½ hours

2 cups full-fat dried milk powder (full-fat dry milk)
⅓ cup granulated sugar

150 ml/¼ pt/small pot of whipping cream
4 tbsp unsalted pistachio nuts, roughly crushed

1 Thoroughly mix together the milk powder, sugar and cream in a microwaveable dish.

2 Microwave on Medium for 2–3 minutes.

3 Remove from the microwave and add two-thirds of the crushed pistachios. Mix together and cook for a further 1–2 minutes.

4 Remove from the microwave and pour into a small rectangular dish. Allow to cool and set.

5 When cold, sprinkle the remaining crushed pistachios over, cut into small pieces and serve.

SERVING SUGGESTIONS AND TIPS

• To make Badam Ki Barfi, substitute almonds for the pistachio.

Pineh Ki Cheej

SOMETHING TO DRINK

There is a wide array of Indian drinks on offer, most of them non-alcoholic. Indians tend to enjoy sweetened drinks so they generally drink sharbhat – sweetened fruit juices in water – or hot, frothy milk served with snacks. The frothiness of milk drinks is created by pouring from one glass to another – an art created and perfected by street vendors. Since the end of the 19th century sweetened tea, with hot frothy milk, has been extremely popular in Indian households.

The drinks in this chapter cover spiced teas, yoghurt drinks (lassi) that can be served at breakfast with crispy flat breads, exotic juicy thirst quenchers, fruity smoothies and milk shakes.

Am Smoothie

MANGO SMOOTHIE

We love the exotically rich yet very refreshing flavour of mango. Not so long ago mangoes were hard to find, but now you can easily buy them in any major supermarket. When they are ready to eat, they should respond to gentle pressure at the tip, but do handle them gently or they will bruise.

serves 4 | preparation 10 minutes | chilling 5 minutes

2 large, very ripe mangos
3 cups milk
a scoop of vanilla ice-cream (optional)

whipped cream (optional)
chocolate sprinkles (optional)

1 Halve the mangos, remove the stone (pit) and scoop out the flesh. Discard the skin.

2 Place the mango flesh and milk in a blender and whiz for a few seconds until they have combined to form a smooth liquid.

3 Pour into a large jug and chill in the fridge for at least 5 minutes before serving.

4 Pour into tall glasses and serve, if you wish, with ice-cream, whipped cream and/or chocolate sprinkles on the top.

SERVING SUGGESTIONS AND TIPS

- You could use two 350 g/12 oz/medium cans of mango slices instead of using fresh.

Kharbuja Cooler

WATERMELON COOLER

Watermelon is always refreshing in hot weather or after spicy food, and this recipe makes a light and refreshing chilled drink that is a great thirst-quencher.

serves 4–6 | preparation 10 minutes | chilling 5 minutes

1 medium watermelon
2 cups crushed ice
1 orange, sliced

1 lemon, sliced
small sprigs of mint, to decorate

1 Scoop out the watermelon pulp and discard the seeds and skin.

2 Whiz the pulp and half a cup of the crushed ice in a blender for a few seconds.

3 Pour into a large drinking jug and add the remaining ice and the orange and lemon slices.

4 Chill for at least 5 minutes before serving in tall glasses decorated with mint sprigs.

Nimbu Pani

LEMON AND LIME THIRST QUENCHER

The combination of limes and lemons is perfect to give a strong and refreshing flavour, while the lemonade gives it just that little bit of sweetness.

serves 4–6 | preparation 5 minutes | chilling time 5 minutes

2 large lemons, halved
2 large limes, halved
1½ cups good-quality lemonade

4 cups water
about 10 ice cubes

1 Cut one lemon and one lime half into slices and place in a large jug.

2 Squeeze the juice from the remaining lemon and lime halves and pour into the jug.

3 Pour the lemonade and water into the jug, add the ice and give it a good stir.

4 Leave for 5 minutes to allow the ice to kick in before serving in tall glasses

Thandai

INDIAN MILK COOLER

A sweet milk-based thirst quencher blended with almonds and crushed ice, thandai is great in hot weather and seriously unusual and refreshing.

serves 4 | preparation 5 minutes

2¹/₂ **cups semi-skimmed milk**
2 **tsp sugar**
5 **drops of rose water**

2 **tsp ground almonds**
a handful of crushed ice, to serve

1 Whiz together all the ingredients in a blender.
2 Serve in tall glasses with the crushed ice.

SERVING SUGGESTION

• Serve with extra ice cubes, if wished.

Am Ki Lassi

MANGO YOGHURT COOLER

An enticingly cool combination of lush, sweet mango blitzed with creamy yoghurt and milk, this makes a great thirst-quencher that is packed with vitamins.

serves 4 | preparation 5 minutes

2 **large ripe mangos**
450 ml/³/₄ pt/**large pot of plain yoghurt**
1¹/₂ **cups milk**

1–2 **tsp caster (superfine) sugar**
a handful of crushed ice, to serve

1 Peel the mango, discard the stone (pit) and coarsely chop the flesh.
2 Place in a blender with the remaining ingredients and whiz for 1 minute until smooth.
3 Serve in tall glasses with the crushed ice.

Phal Ki Sharbhat

EXOTIC FRUIT QUENCH

An improvised concoction of exotic fruits blended together and served with ice, this makes an exotic, citrussy, thirst-quenching drink. You can alter the combination of fruits according to what is available and experiment to make your own favourite combinations, if you wish.

serves 4 | preparation 10 minutes

1 large ripe mango, peeled and chopped
1 large orange, peeled and segmented
1 satsuma, peeled and segemented

$^1/_2$ **pineapple, chopped**
$^1/_2$ **tsp sugar**
a handful of crushed ice

1 Place all the fruits in a blender and whiz for a few seconds until smooth.

2 Add the sugar and whiz for 1 minute.

3 Put the crushed ice in tall glasses, add the blended fruits and serve straight away.

SERVING SUGGESTIONS AND TIPS

- You could use a 350 g/12 oz/medium can of pineapple slices, chunks or pieces instead of fresh.

- Substitute papaya (pawpaw), or a blend of other fruits of your choice, for the mango.

Namakeen Lassi

SALTED YOGHURT COOLER

A savoury version of a great Punjabi thirst quencher, this is both our dads' favourite drink, accompanied by parathas or by itself as a mid-morning snack. Cool, mild yoghurt simply combined with toasted cumin seeds and salt, it is just the right thing to slake your thirst and satisfying enough to set you up for the rest of the day.

serves 4 | preparation 5 minutes

1 tsp cumin seeds
450 ml/³/₄ pt/large pot of plain yoghurt
1¹/₂ cups milk

1 tsp salt
a handful of crushed ice, to serve

1 Dry-roast the cumin seeds in a frying pan (skillet) for 1 minute until they begin to pop. Allow to cool a little, then put them between two pieces of kitchen paper (paper towels) and crush to a coarse powder with the flat end of a rolling pin.

2 Place in a blender with the yoghurt, milk, salt and half the cumin and whiz for 1 minute.

3 Serve chilled in tall glasses with crushed ice and the remaining cumin sprinkled over.

SERVING SUGGESTIONS AND TIPS

- As a variation, substitute ¹/₄ tsp freshly ground black pepper and ¹/₂ tsp rose water for the cumin seeds.

Badam te Pista Dudh

ALMOND AND PISTACHIO MILK SHAKE

A great Indian milk shake, this is made with the delicious combination of blanched almonds and pistachios scented with fragrant cardamom. You can use ready-made ground cardamom or remove the seeds from pods and grind them yourself using a pestle and mortar.

serves 4 | preparation 5 minutes

2¹/₂ **cups semi-skimmed milk**
2 **tsp sugar**
5 **tbsp blanched almonds**
¹/₂ **tsp ground cardamom (from about**
  5 **whole green pods)**

5 **tbsp unsalted pistachio nuts**
¹/₂ **tsp rose water (optional)**
a handful of crushed ice, to serve

1   Place the milk, sugar, almonds, cardamom, pistachios and rose water, if using, in a blender and whiz until smooth.

2   Serve in tall glasses with a handful of crushed ice.

SERVING SUGGESTIONS AND TIPS

- You can omit the pistachios if you prefer.
- Omit the ice and boil the blended ingredients for 5 minutes to make a hot nightcap.

Masala Chai

SPICED TEA

Tea is made in almost every Indian household several times a day, from first thing in the morning on its own to afternoon tea with samosas and fritters (pakorae). In our houses it seems to be made almost every hour! The spices used in this tea are good for upset stomachs and to encourage general health.

serves 4 | preparation 5 minutes | brewing 5 minutes

3 **tea bags**
6 **cardamom pods, split**
6 **whole cloves**
¹/₂ **tsp fennel seeds**

5 **cm/2 in cinnamon stick**
3 **cups water**
3 **cups milk**
sugar to taste (optional)

1 Place the all the ingredients except the milk in a saucepan. Bring to the boil and boil for 1 minute so the flavours all mix.

2 Add the milk, return to the boil, then reduce the heat and simmer for 1 minute.

3 Strain through with a tea strainer and pour into cups.

4 Add sugar according to taste, if you wish.

SERVING SUGGESTION

- Enjoy with hot spicy fritters, such as Etwar Ki Aloo Palak Pakorae (see page 27) or Mummji's Alaag Aloo Tikkis (see page 22), or try it with something sweet, such as Pista Dudh Ki Barfi (see page 123).

Elachi Chai

CARDAMON TEA

This delicious tea is made with ordinary tea bags flavoured with cardamom pods. They impart a delicious aniseedy flavour to the tea, which not only tastes great but is good for the digestion. You can buy cardamom pods in any supermarket or Indian store and we use them a lot in our cooking so they won't be wasted!

serves 4 | preparation 5 minutes | brewing 5 minutes

3 tea bags
6 cardamom pods, split
3 cups water

1 cup milk
sugar to taste (optional)

1 Place the tea bags, cardamom and water in a saucepan. Bring to the boil and boil for 1 minute so the flavours all mix.

2 Add the milk, return to the boil, then reduce the heat and simmer for 1–2 minutes.

3 Strain through with tea strainer and pour into cups.

4 Add sugar according to taste, if you wish.

SERVING SUGGESTIONS

- Enjoy simply by itself or with any Indian snacks or sweets.

Chat Pata Ki Cheej

SOMETHING TANGY

Chutneys and pickles are a bonus to an Indian meal, giving your taste buds that extra tingle. They are delicious with any curry and are very popular served with breads such as parathas (see pages 106 and 108–110) to make a complete meal.

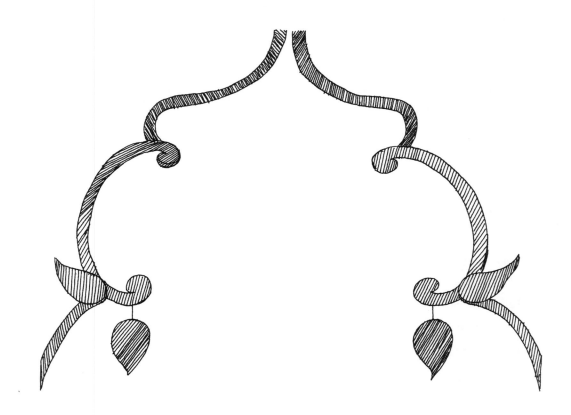

Mr T's Tazhee Pudina Chutney

MR T'S FRESH MINT CHUTNEY

This chutney recipe is famously made by Babita's dear father-in-law, Mr T. It's all the family's favourite as its unique flavour of mint, apples, chilli, lemon juice and coriander makes it so mouth-wateringly tempting. Three chillies will give you a hot chutney; you can use more or fewer to suit your taste.

serves 4–6 | preparation 10 minutes

3 large handfuls of fresh mint
2 tsp mint sauce
2 tsp garden mint sauce
1 large Granny Smith or other sharp
  eating (dessert) apple
2 large onions, roughly chopped
2 garlic cloves
3 green finger chillies, seeded

$1/2$ tsp ground cumin
1 tsp salt
juice of 1 lemon
a large handful of fresh coriander
  (cilantro)
1 tbsp water
a sprig of coriander, to garnish

1 Place all the ingredients except the water in a blender or grinder and whiz until the ingredients are blended. Add enough of the water, a little at a time, until a nicely textured paste is formed.

2 Transfer to a serving dish and garnish with a sprig of fresh coriander.

SERVING SUGGESTIONS AND TIPS

- A must-have for dipping your Sunday afternoon samosae and pakorae in.
- When using chillies in these recipes, remember that 1 = mild, 2 = medium, 3 = hot, 4 = very hot.

Sukha Naryial Hare Mirch Chutney

COCONUT GREEN CHILLI CHUTNEY

This is one of Leela Auntie's many specialities. It's her delicious version of a chutney made with plenty of rich coconut and hot green chillies that's commonly prepared in South Indian cooking. It goes particularly well with any of our vegetarian snacks (see pages 21–33).

serves 4–6 | preparation 10 minutes

½ fresh or dried coconut, grated
5 cm/2 in piece of root ginger, peeled
2 green finger chillies, seeded
1 tsp salt
4 tbsp yoghurt

juice of 2 limes
3 tbsp olive or sunflower oil
1½ tsp mustard seeds
2 or 3 curry leaves
2 red chillies

1　Grind the coconut, ginger and green chillies in a blender. If you are using fresh coconut, add the coconut milk. Add the salt, yoghurt and lime juice.

2　Heat the oil, add the mustard seeds, curry leaves and whole red chillies and fry (sauté) for 2–3 minutes. Add to the blended ingredients.

3　Transfer to a serving dish and serve.

Khatti Mithi Imli Ki Chutney

TANGY TAMARIND CHUTNEY

The combination of tamarind and ketchup gives this a mouth-watering tangy flavour. A very popular chutney and one that makes a delicious accompaniment, particularly to samosae, pakorae, Dahi Wale Punjabi Chole (see page 23) and Mummyji's Alaag Aloo Tikkis (see page 22).

serves 6–8 | preparation 5 minutes | cooking 10 minutes

2 tbsp sugar
1 cup water
1 tsp tamarind paste
2–3 tbsp tomato ketchup (catsup)
2–3 tbsp brown sauce
1 tsp mint sauce

1 carrot, grated
1 small onion, chopped
1 tbsp garam masala
2 green finger chillies, chopped
1 tsp salt

1. Place the sugar and water in a saucepan and boil until the sugar dissolves. Allow to cool for 10 minutes.

2. Mix all the remaining ingredients into the cooled syrup.

3. Transfer to a serving bowl, cover and chill. It will keep in the fridge for up to 3 days.

SERVING SUGGESTIONS AND TIPS

- Serve as an accompaniment to any starter, particularly vegetable-based ones.

Piyaz, Tomater te Hari Mirch

ONION, TOMATO AND CHILLI RELISH

A chunky tangy chilli relish, this is flavoured with rich tomatoes, spices and chillies. Use one chilli for a mild relish, two for medium, three for hot or four for very hot, according to your taste. The mint gives it a final lift and perfectly complements the hot flavours.

serves 4–6 | preparation 10 minutes

1 large onion, roughly chopped
6 tomatoes, roughly chopped
2 green finger chillies, seeded
2–3 tbsp water
$^1/_2$ tsp salt
1 tsp garam masala

$^1/_2$ tsp freshly ground black pepper
$^1/_2$ tsp paprika
$^1/_2$ tsp sugar
a handful of fresh mint
a sprig of mint, to garnish

1. Using a blender, roughly grind the onion, tomatoes and chillies, adding enough of the water, a little at a time, until you obtain a chunky-textured paste.

2. Add the garam masala, salt, pepper, paprika, sugar and mint and blend for a further 10 seconds.

3. Transfer to a serving dish and garnish with a sprig of mint.

SERVING SUGGESTIONS AND TIPS

- Great for dipping your samosae in.

- You could use a 400 g/14 oz/large can of tomatoes instead of fresh.

Tarwala Dahi

CUCUMBER RAITA

Tarwala Dahi is a cooling creamy yoghurt dish mixed with grated cucumber, which makes a fantastic flavour and texture combination. Serve it with any spicy meat or vegetarian curries to take away the heat and offer a lovely cooling contrast.

serves 4–6 | preparation 5 minutes

450 ml/³/₄ pt/large pot of plain low-fat yoghurt
¹/₂ cup milk

¹/₂ cucumber, grated
¹/₄ tsp salt
¹/₂ tsp freshly ground black pepper

1 Empty the yoghurt into a bowl. Add the milk and stir vigorously until the yoghurt is evenly thinned out.

2 Stir in the cucumber.

3 Add the salt and pepper, stir well and serve.

Pudina Dahi

MINT SAUCE YOGHURT

A smooth and cooling concoction of mint and yoghurt, this is usually served with starters and snacks. Its refreshing tanginess tickles the taste buds and enhances your enjoyment of whatever you eat with it. It makes a great accompaniment to all kinds of Indian dishes.

serves 4–6 | preparation 5 minutes

150 ml/¹/₄ pt/small pot of plain low-fat yoghurt
¹/₄ cup milk
¹/₂ tsp salt salt

1¹/₂ tbsp mint sauce
³/₄ tsp sugar (optional)
a few sprigs of mint, to garnish

1 Combine all the ingredients.

2 Transfer to a serving dish and garnish with sprigs of mint.

Gajar Ka Achar

CARROT PICKLE

Fresh, crunchy carrots spiced up with fennel and chillies create this simple, zingy pickle to complement any Indian curry or other dish. It takes hardly any time and really tastes so much more authentic when you make your own rather than relying on ready-made pickles.

makes about 20 servings | **preparation 10 minutes** | **cooking 5 minutes**

5 tbsp sunflower oil
1 tbsp Indian whole pickling spice (optional)
1 tsp salt
1½ tsp turmeric

1 tbsp fennel seeds
4 carrots, finely chopped
2 green finger chillies, finely sliced
2 tbsp lemon juice

1 Heat the oil in a saucepan over a medium heat and toss in the pickling spice, if using, salt, tumeric, fennel seeds and carrots. Cook for 3 minutes until softened.

2 Allow to cool a little, then add the chillies and lemon juice

3 Transfer to a clean airtight jar. Leave for at least a week to allow the flavours to develop, shaking the jar once or twice a day. Eat within 1 month.

SERVING SUGGESTIONS AND TIPS

- Great for eating with buttered crispy flat breads (see pages 106 and 108–110) or any curry.

- Add a a little thinly sliced root ginger with the carrots to make the pickle even tastier.

Masala Dahi

SPICED YOGHURT

A cooling yet spicy yoghurt dish flavoured with paprika and garam masala, this is guaranteed to get your taste buds tingling.

serves 4–6 | preparation 5 minutes

450 ml/³/₄ pt/large pot of plain low-fat yoghurt
¹/₂ cup milk
¹/₂ tsp salt

¹/₂ tsp freshly ground black pepper
¹/₂ tsp garam masala
¹/₂ tsp paprika

1 Empty the yoghurt into a bowl. Add the milk and stir vigorously until the yoghurt is evenly thinned out.

2 Mix in the salt.

3 Sprinkle all the remaining spices on the surface of the yoghurt in a pattern of your choice before serving. Don't stir it in as it will look and taste great.

SERVING SUGGESTIONS AND TIPS

- Babita's father-in-law – Mr T – enjoys this dish as a starter with a fresh mixed salad and his Tazhee Pudina Chutney (see page 133).

Tomater te Piyaz Dahi

TOMATO AND ONION YOGHURT

A crunchy onion and colourful tomato spicy yoghurt dish flavoured with paprika and garam masala, this makes an ideal accompaniment to any curry, or a starter with popadoms to get your taste buds tingling and get you ready for your main course. Serve it with grilled dishes, too.

serves 4–6 | preparation 5 minutes

1 tbsp cumin seeds (optional)
450 ml/³/₄ pt/large pot of plain low-fat yoghurt
¹/₂ cup milk

¹/₂ tsp garam masala
¹/₂ tsp salt
1 large tomato, diced
1 small onion, diced

1 Dry-roast the cumin seeds in a frying pan (skillet) for 1 minute until they begin to pop.

2 Empty the yoghurt into a bowl. Add the milk and stir vigorously until yoghurt is evenly thinned out.

3 Mix in the garam masala, salt, tomato and onion.

4 Sprinkle the cumin seeds on the surface of the yoghurt in a pattern of your choice before serving. Don't stir it in as it will look and taste great.

SERVING SUGGESTIONS AND TIPS

- Serve with any curry.

Seb Achar

APPLE PICKLE

Fresh, crunchy green apple chunks spiced up with salt and chillies create this simple zingy pickle to complement any Indian curry or other dish. As always, you can adjust the number of chillies to suit your taste. We suggest two for medium, and three or even four if you like it a bit hotter.

makes about 8 servings | preparation 10 minutes | cooking 5 minutes

2 tbsp olive oil
2–4 green finger chillies, chopped
2 tsp salt

¹/₂ tsp garam masala (optional)
2 large cooking (tart) apples, cut into 2.5 cm/1 inch chunks

1 Heat the oil in a frying pan (skillet) for 1 minute. Add the chillies, salt, garam masala, if using, and apples and cook gently for 2–3 minutes, stirring occasionally to mix in all the ingredients.

2 Remove from the heat and serve straight away. Alternatively, allow to cool enough to transfer to a securely sealed glass jar and keep in the fridge for up to 3 days.

SERVING SUGGESTIONS AND TIPS

- Great for eating with buttered crispy flat breads (see pages 106 and 108–110) or any curry.

Nimbu Ka Achar

LEMON PICKLE

This is a deliciously sharp pickle that cuts through and complements spicy flavours and fried dishes especially well. You can buy mustard oil in most ethnic stores or in major supermarkets. If you would like an oil-free version, try the variation below.

makes about 18 servings | **preparation 10 minutes** | **cooking 5 minutes**

6 lemons
1 cup mustard oil
2 or 3 x 5 cm/2 in pieces of root ginger, peeled and sliced lengthways

2 tsp salt
½ cup pickling vinegar
6 green finger chillies, sliced lengthways (optional)

1 Wash and dry the lemons and slice into wedges.

2 Heat the oil and cook the ginger for 2 minutes over a low heat.

3 Add the lemon wedges, salt and chillies, if using, and cook for 1 minute.

4 Remove from the heat and allow to cool.

5 Transfer to an airtight jar and top up with the pickling vinegar. Leave for a week to allow the flavours to develop, shaking the jar once or twice a day. Use within 1 month.

SERVING SUGGESTIONS AND TIPS

- Great for eating with buttered crispy flat breads (see pages 106 and 108–10), or any curry.

- Substitute 9 limes for the lemons to make Kacha Nimbu Ka Achar.

- For Bally Auntiji's drier, oil-free pickle, soak the lemons overnight in water. Dry with a tea towel (dish cloth) and cut into wedges. Place in an airtight jar and add 6 green finger chillies, sliced lengthways, 1 tbsp salt, 1 tsp turmeric and 1 tbsp Indian whole pickling spice. Mix together, then leave for a week, shaking the jar once or twice a day, to allow the flavours to develop. Use within 1 month.

Khajur te Sogia Ka Pickle

DATE AND SULTANA PICKLE

We love this traditionally rich, fruity pickle, dense-textured and dark in colour –
absolutely delicious served with spicy curries or with a selection of pickles and breads
as a starter or dip. As it is made as a traditional preserve it keeps well, so it's a good
pickle to make even if you don't want to serve it to many guests at a time.

makes about 8 servings | preparation 10 minutes | cooking 5 minutes

1 tbsp fennel seeds or Indian whole
   pickling spice
2 tbsp olive oil
1 cup dried dates, chopped and stoned
   (pitted)

¼ cup pickling vinegar
1 cup sultanas (golden raisins)
1 tbsp salt
1 tbsp freshly ground black pepper

1 Place the fennel seeds or pickling spice in a saucepan, add the oil and fry (sauté)
   over a medium heat for 1 minute.

2 Add all the remaining ingredients, mix together and cook until all the liquid has
   absorbed. Remove from the heat to cool.

3 Mix thoroughly and transfer to an airtight jar. Use within 1 month.

SERVING SUGGESTIONS AND TIPS

- Great for eating with buttered crispy flat breads (see pages 106 and 108–10),
  or any curry.

On-line Resources

If you are unable to buy your spices locally, try contacting these mail-order suppliers.

Bristol Sweet Mart
80 St Mark's Road
Bristol
BS5 6JH
Tel +44 (0) 1179 512257
Fax +44 (0) 1179 52545
E-mail: sales@sweetmart.co.uk
Website:
www.sweetmart.co.uk/index.htm

Get Spice Ltd
Website:
www.getspice.com

In2Curry
Kingfield Road
Coventry
West Midlands CV1 4DW
Tel: +44 (0) 2476 630635
Fax: +44 (0) 2476 630628
E-mail: enquiries@in2curry.co.uk
Website: www.in2curry.co.uk

Natco Foods Limited
Website: www.natco-online.com/

Simply Spice
Website:
www.simplyspice.co.uk

The Spice Shop
1 Blenheim Crescent
London W11 2EE
Tel: +44 (0) 20 7221 4448
E-mail: enquires@thespiceshop.co.uk
Website:
www.thespiceshoponline.com

Index